DANIEL A. PAYNE
GREAT BLACK LEADER

RUDINE SIMS BISHOP

SCHOLASTIC INC.
New York   Toronto   London   Auckland
Sydney   New Delhi   Hong Kong

Dedication

Honoring my first church home
Bethel AME Church, Pottsville, PA

Where Bishop Payne once stopped by and left a lasting impression

Credits appear on page 67, which constitutes an extension of this copyright page.

Text copyright © 2009 by Rudine Sims Bishop.
All rights reserved. Published by Scholastic Inc., 557 Broadway, New York, NY 10012, by arrangement with Just Us Books.
Printed in the U.S.A.

ISBN-13: 978-0-545-27458-6
ISBN-10: 0-545-27458-3

SCHOLASTIC and associated logos and designs are trademarks and/or registered trademarks of Scholastic Inc.

2 3 4 5 6 7 8 9 10   23   19 18 17 16 15 14 13 12 11

CONTENTS

FOREWORD

Rudine Sims Bishop has written a book that is not only appropriate for the time in which Daniel Payne lived, but also for the Obama era of which we are now all a part. Bishop Daniel Payne: Great Black Leader is a significant work because it captures the life of one of the world's most extraordinary human beings. Bishop Payne has often been defined by his role in founding America's first university owned and operated by African Americans. The impact of this singular event has spawned generations of young people who otherwise would not have had an opportunity to participate in higher learning.

Payne's tenacity was reflected not only in his focus on higher education in general, but also in the preparation of young men who occupied various pulpits. These were persons who often came off plantations, where they had been denied, by virtue of race, access to the White institutions that existed. As they were educated, it created a rift in the AME Church; bishops debated issues regarding the free form worship that slaves practiced and the literary form of worship of formally educated Blacks. The remnants of that battle are still evident as some members of the AME Church seek a quiet, low-toned worship experience while others prefer a more spirited, lively style of worship.

Payne truly believed that God had called him for the work of teaching and it was exemplified in his testimony. He proclaimed the Lord revealed to him: "I have set thee apart to educate thyself in order that thou mayest be an educator to thy people." By every definition Bishop Payne was not simply a teacher, but a very extraordinary one, taking the time to teach himself Greek, Latin, geography, map-making, English grammar, mathematics and science.

With so much focus today on what Barack Obama's election means, it is good to know that preceding him was Daniel Payne, on whose shoulders President Obama stands. Times have changed, but African Americans are still in need of knowledge about Daniel Payne, whose life is a textbook on excellence. The African Methodist Episcopal Church and Wilberforce University represent significant building blocks that allowed African Americans in the post-slave era to dare to dream. More than dreams, they were hallmarks of hope for people who could have easily given up. Change as we know it today may well have sprouted from the roots that were planted by Daniel Alexander Payne. I am proud to have had the opportunity to walk in his foot path by serving as the 18th President of Wilberforce University, which still stands as a center of hope, promise and possibility for this and future generations.

—The Honorable Reverend Floyd H. Flake, D. Min.
Pastor, Greater Allen A.M.E. Cathedral of New York,
Retired U.S. Congressman

PREFACE

While doing research for a book on African-American children's literature, I learned that some of the earliest writing for children by African Americans can be found in church publications. The name of one church leader, Bishop Daniel Alexander Payne of the African Methodist Episcopal (AME) Church, kept turning up in discussions of these publications and of efforts to educate African Americans in the 1800s. As I discovered more information about Bishop Payne, I was captivated by the life story of this five-foot, 100-pound little giant who rose from an orphaned carpenter's apprentice, to a bishop, to president of the first African-American university and one of the most influential African-American leaders of the nineteenth century. He was a contemporary of Abraham Lincoln and Frederick Douglass, and he interacted with both of them as well as with numerous other well-known American and European leaders. Although his family was free, he was born in Charleston, South Carolina at a time when most African Americans were being held in slavery, and the laws of the land kept slavery and discrimination legal. When I read about his efforts to teach himself, his crusade for education for African Americans, his leadership roles, and his determination to hold to and share his religious faith—all in spite of the many obstacles placed in his path—I was convinced he was someone today's young people would like to know about. When I discovered that Bishop

Payne had once visited the little AME church in Pottsville, Pennsylvania where I grew up, I felt that I was the one who should tell his story.

This book would not have been possible, however, without the aid and support of several people. First I want to thank my publishers Cheryl and Wade Hudson for expressing interest in the book even before it was written and for helping to make it better than it was when they first saw the manuscript. Thanks to Miss Jacqueline Brown, archivist at the Wilberforce University Library, for making the library's archival materials on Bishop Payne accessible to me, and for securing copies of important images. I also thank Ohio State University colleagues Dr. Susan Fisher and Dr. Barbara Bloettschner, of the Department of Entomology, who provided information that allowed me to identify the caterpillar that, in Bishop Payne's view, led to some life-changing events. I am grateful to Dr. Ricardo Bessin, Dept. of Entomology at the University of Kentucky, who promptly and generously gave me permission to use, without a fee, his beautiful color photograph of a cecropia moth caterpillar. Dr. Pete Yasenchak, of the Schuylkill County Historical Society searched for a photograph of Bethel AME Church in Pottsville, PA and, in the absence of a suitable photograph in his files, asked his wife to go out and take some photographs, which they sent to me by e-mail on the very day that I called. Thanks to him and to Mrs. Yasenchak. And finally, my eternal gratitude to my husband, one-man support team, and favorite photographer, Dr. James J. Bishop, who drove to Wilberforce and Payne Theological Seminary with me and took numerous photographs, including the one that forms the backdrop for a number of images in the book.

–Rudine Sims Bishop
March 16, 2009

The Battery in Charleston, South Carolina. During the early nineteenth century, Charleston was the cultural and economic center of the South. It was a busy seaport, a major center for the slave trade, and a summer resort for wealthy planters with big city homes.

CHARLESTON, SOUTH CAROLINA

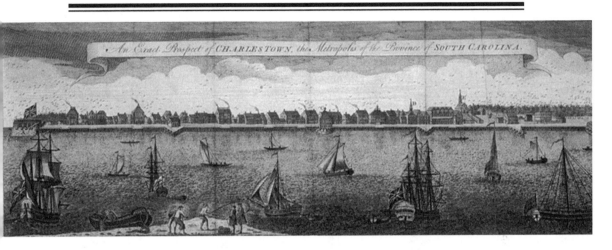

"I was the child of many prayers."
—Daniel A. Payne, *Recollections of Seventy Years*

RIDING HIGH on his father's shoulders, little Daniel Alexander Payne had a breathtaking view of the excitement. Lights were shining all over Charleston, South Carolina. The War of 1812 had ended and the city was celebrating the peace. Daniel was about four years old, and this special moment with his father was one of his earliest and happiest memories. It must have been a happy time for his father, too. London Payne, who was a man of faith and a leader in his church, believed that Daniel was the answer to his prayers. He had very much wanted a son, and he had promised that if his baby were a boy, he would dedicate the child to God and name him after the prophet Daniel from the Bible. Little Daniel was born on February 24,

1

1811, and soon after that, London Payne dedicated his son to God twice—once when Daniel was baptized in church, and again right after the ceremony, at their home on Swinton Lane in Charleston.

Charleston was a bustling center of trade and commerce, and home to thousands of Black people. In fact, Black people made up the majority of the city's population, even though most of them were being held in slavery. Charleston's prosperity depended on slave labor. Enslaved workers harvested the rice and cotton on nearby plantations, loaded and unloaded ships in the busy harbor, and helped to build new ships. Yet these all-important workers were considered property, like mules or farmland. They had no rights and few opportunities, and they were hungry for freedom and for knowledge that would help them make their lives better. Charleston was also home to many free persons of color—Black people who were not enslaved. Many of them were skilled workers who made a decent living, but they, too, were hungry for education. Some of them even set up schools for fellow Blacks, both free and enslaved.

London Payne and his family were legally free, and therefore

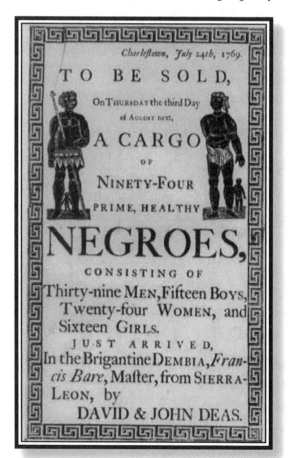

A broadside advertising the sale of ninety-four newly arrived Africans in Charleston. They would become slaves.

DANIEL A. PAYNE

better off than many of their Black neighbors. But he knew what it was to be enslaved. He had been born free in Virginia, but when he was just a young boy, some sailors had kidnapped him, taken him to Charleston, and sold him as a slave to a man who painted signs and houses. When London was grown he had to pay a thousand dollars to buy the freedom that was already rightfully his. Because he knew the importance of education, he started teaching his son the alphabet and

Silhouette of Martha Payne.

some beginning reading when Daniel was only three or four. It was one of the last things London Payne was able to do for his son. He died when Daniel was about four and a half years old.

Daniel's mother, Martha Payne, was Catawba Indian and Black. She was a gentle woman with a pleasant personality and deep religious faith. After her husband died, Martha often took her little Daniel by the hand and led him to the Methodist church, where he sat beside her listening to the service. This lasted only about five years, for when Daniel was about nine and a half years old, Martha

ACCORDING TO THE UNITED STATES CENSUS BUREAU, IN 1810, THE YEAR BEFORE DANIEL PAYNE WAS BORN, THERE WERE 1,191,362 BLACK AMERICANS HELD IN SLAVERY. IN CHARLESTON THERE WERE 11,568 WHITES, 11,671 SLAVES AND 1,472 FREE PEOPLE OF COLOR. THE POPULATION OF FREE BLACK AMERICANS WAS 186,446.

Payne died of tuberculosis. But with their strong faith and their great respect for learning, Martha and London Payne had introduced Daniel to the two big passions of his life—religion and education.

With Martha's death Daniel had become an orphan, but he did have an older married sister and a great-aunt, Sarah Bordeaux. Aunt Sarah took him in and cared for him as if he were her own son. For two years Daniel attended a school established for poor and orphaned Black children by the Minor's Moralist Society, a group of free men of color. After that, he attended the most popular "colored" school in the city, run by Thomas Bonneau. Daniel was probably one of the smallest boys in his age group, but when it came to learning, he was a champion. He was almost always at the head of his class. By the time he was twelve, Daniel had learned about as much as Mr. Bonneau's school could teach him, and it was time to learn a trade. For four

IN 1822, WHEN DANIEL WAS ELEVEN YEARS OLD, DENMARK VESEY, A FREE BLACK CARPENTER AND A LEADER IN CHARLESTON'S AFRICAN METHODIST EPISCOPAL CHURCH, PLANNED A LARGE AND SOPHISTICATED SLAVE REVOLT. A NERVOUS SLAVE BETRAYED THE PLOT AND VESEY AND HIS FELLOW REBELS WERE HANGED BEFORE THEY COULD CARRY IT OUT. VESEY'S CHURCH WAS BURNED DOWN. HIS PASTOR WAS THE REV. MORRIS BROWN, WHO ESCAPED FROM CHARLESTON AND LATER BECAME THE SECOND BISHOP IN THE AME CHURCH. THE 56 BULL STREET RESIDENCE IN CHARLESTON (ABOVE) IS BELIEVED TO BE THE HOME OF DENMARK VESEY.

DANIEL A. PAYNE

and a half years he was an apprentice to his sister's husband, James Holloway, who was a carpenter. For Daniel, the best thing about working with his brother-in-law was that while he was learning carpentry, he could also make time to read. One day he came across a book that "became the turning point" of his life. The author was the Rev. John Brown, a minister from Scotland, who wrote that he had taught himself to read Latin, Greek, and Hebrew. Daniel thought, "If Brown learned Latin, Greek, and Hebrew without a living teacher, why can't

Toussaint L'Ouverture, Haiti's revolutionary leader, was Daniel's childhood hero.

I?" He decided to try, and thanks to the Rev. Brown's example, Daniel became a lifelong autodidact, a person who teaches himself.

He began by reading every book he could get his hands on. Like many young boys, he especially enjoyed the stories of men of action. He admired freedom fighters such as Robert the Bruce and William Wallace (Brave Heart), who had fought for Scotland's freedom from England. But his main hero was Toussaint L'Ouverture, a Black man who led the fight to free Black people in Haiti from slavery. Daniel thought he too would become a soldier and go fight with the Haitian people. But one night in a dream he became a fighting soldier, witnessing the terrible sights and hearing the awful sounds of battle. He was horrified; the dream showed him that he could never be a soldier at war.

When he was about seventeen, Daniel realized what he was meant to do instead. As his parents had taught him, he had made prayer a part of his daily life. Even when he was a child, he had prayed often, asking God to make him a good boy. One day he was in his room praying, when suddenly he felt as if hands were pressing down on his shoulders, and a voice deep inside was saying, "I have set thee apart to educate thyself in order that thou mayest be an educator to thy people." He believed it was the voice of God, calling him to teach.

Before he would start to teach others, though, Daniel worked even harder at educating himself. He spent all his spare money buying books, and all his spare time studying. He earned book money by making "tables, benches, clothes-horses, and corset-bones," which he sold in the public market on Saturday nights. During the week at mealtime, he would eat as quickly as he could and use the rest of the time to read. After work he would read until midnight. Then he would get up at four o'clock in the morning and read by candlelight. He not only read books, he also drew pictures and wrote poetry. He would read, write and draw for two hours, until six, when it was time to go to work in the carpenter shop. Daniel followed this self-made schedule as strictly as a soldier following orders. Even though he must have been exhausted some days, he kept to it until he felt ready to answer the call to teach.

FREE PEOPLE OF COLOR

By the 1800s, thousands of free people of color were living in cities such as Charleston. Many made a living in trades such as barbering (left), carpentry, and tailoring. In 1838, a Philadelphia abolitionist group reported (below) that, in spite of discrimination, the city's free people of color owned property, paid taxes, and looked after each other's welfare.

Charleston "Free Badge"
From 1783 to 1789 in Charleston all free persons of color fifteen and older were required to buy from the city and wear a copper badge like the one above. It shows a "liberty hat" on a pole.

THE

PRESENT STATE AND CONDITION

OF THE

FREE PEOPLE OF COLOR,

OF THE

CITY OF PHILADELPHIA

AND

ADJOINING DISTRICTS, AS EXHIBITED BY THE

REPORT

OF A

COMMITTEE OF THE PENNSYLVANIA SOCIETY

FOR

PROMOTING THE ABOLITION OF SLAVERY, &c.

Read First Month (Jan.) 5th, 1838.

PHILADELPHIA:
PUBLISHED BY THE SOCIETY.
MERRIHEW AND GUNN, PRINTERS,
No. 7 Carter's Alley.
1838.

Zion School for Colored Children, Charleston, 1866. After the Civil War, freed African Americans flocked to schools like this, established by the government and churches. Before then free people of color, especially in the South, had to provide their own schools.

TWO: 1829-1835
A LIVING TEXTBOOK,
AN EXTRAORDINARY TEACHER

"Pursue knowledge wherever it is to be found. Like the air you breathe, it may be inhaled everywhere."
advice from John Bachman as Daniel Payne was leaving Charleston.
—Daniel A. Payne, *Recollections of Seventy Years*

DANIEL WAS 18 when he opened his first school. It was only one room in the home of Caesar Wright, and there were only six students. During the day he taught Mr. Wright's three children, and at night he taught three enslaved adults. He charged 50¢ a month for each student, but $3.00 a month was not nearly enough to live on. After about a year of struggling to make ends meet, he closed the school and started searching for another way to make a living. He went to see a rich slaveholder who was looking to hire a free young Black man to go to the West Indies with him and help with his business. Trying to persuade Daniel to take the job, the slaveholder asked, "Daniel, do you know what makes the difference between master and servant?" Answering his own question, he continued, "Nothing but superior knowledge—nothing but one man knowing more than another. Now, if you will go with me, the knowledge you

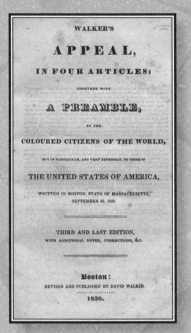

WALKER'S
APPEAL,
IN FOUR ARTICLES;

TOGETHER WITH

A PREAMBLE,

TO THE

COLOURED CITIZENS OF THE WORLD,

BUT IN PARTICULAR, AND VERY EXPRESSLY, TO THOSE OF

THE UNITED STATES OF AMERICA,

WRITTEN IN BOSTON, STATE OF MASSACHUSETTS,
SEPTEMBER 28, 1829.

THIRD AND LAST EDITION,
WITH ADDITIONAL NOTES, CORRECTIONS, &c.

Boston:
REVISED AND PUBLISHED BY DAVID WALKER.
1830.

THE SAME YEAR DANIEL OPENED HIS SCHOOL, 1829, DAVID WALKER, A FREE BLACK MAN LIVING IN BOSTON, PUBLISHED HIS *APPEAL*, (LEFT). THIS PAMPHLET ATTACKED SLAVERY AND URGED SLAVES IN THE UNITED STATES OF AMERICA TO REVOLT. WALKER USED SAILORS TO SEND AND DISTRIBUTE COPIES OF HIS PAMPHLET IN THE SOUTHERN STATES. THIS ANGERED SLAVEHOLDERS AND THEIR SUPPORTERS. WALKER WAS FOUND DEAD AT HIS HOME IN 1830, BUT HIS *APPEAL* CONTINUED TO INSPIRE ENSLAVED AND FREE BLACKS TO AGITATE FOR THE ABOLITION OF SLAVERY FOR YEARS AFTER HIS DEATH.

ONE OF THE FIRST SCHOOLS TO EDUCATE BLACKS WAS THE NEW YORK AFRICAN FREE SCHOOL (RIGHT), ESTABLISHED IN 1787. THIS SKETCH WAS DRAWN BY PATRICK REASON, A 13-YEAR OLD STUDENT.

may acquire will be of more value to you than the money you will earn." Right then Daniel understood what people meant when they said, "knowledge is power." He was inspired—not to go with the slaveholder, but to go after more knowledge. He was determined to gain as much knowledge as the slaveholders had, and he intended to share his knowledge with as many Black people as he could reach.

Daniel re-opened his school, and this time it was a big success. He continued to teach himself—Greek and Latin, geography, map-making, English grammar, mathematics, and science. He was curious about everything, in one case perhaps too curious. On February 12, 1831 the sky over Charleston turned dark in the middle of the day. The moon passed between the earth and the sun, causing a total solar eclipse. Daniel could not resist studying this rare event.

DANIEL A. PAYNE

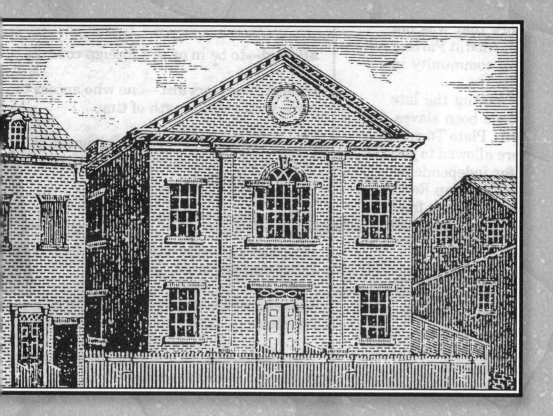

He watched the eclipse with his naked eye, which was a terrible mistake. During an eclipse the light from the sun is so concentrated that it can cause blindness by burning the retina in the back of the eye. It is like using a magnifying glass to burn a piece of paper by focusing the sun's rays on one spot. For three weeks after the eclipse, Daniel could not read at all; every time he opened a book the pages looked like black sheets. Eventually he was able to read again, but he never fully recovered his eyesight.

All his reading and studying probably made Daniel the best-educated "colored" teacher in Charleston. He may also have been the most enthusiastic. He loved teaching, and his students caught his excitement. His school soon became the most popular of the five "colored" schools in the city; it grew to about sixty students. Twice

Dr. John Bachman, a Lutheran minister and naturalist, was a major influence on Daniel during his early years as a teacher. Dr. Bachman was well known for his collaboration with John James Audubon and wrote the text for Audubon's illustrations in the book, The Quadrapeds of North America. *Dr. Bachman was the founder of Newberry College in South Carolina and a man of great stature and influence in the Luthern Church.*

he had to move to larger spaces, the last time to a school that had been built especially for him. He became so well known that two teachers from other schools in the city came to him to learn science. He willingly shared his knowledge.

Daniel's school was probably just one large room. There were few, if any textbooks, but Daniel himself was a living textbook, and he brought the natural world into his classroom. On Saturdays he and some of the boys in his class would go into the woods to search for plants and animals to bring back to the school. He taught his students how to draw flowers, fruit and animals on paper and on velvet cloth. He collected insects, toads, snakes, young alligators, fish and young sharks for his students to study. He cleaned and preserved the animals, then hung them on the classroom walls. Daniel even cooked and tasted the meat of the animals he captured— all except toads and snakes—so he could learn as much as possible about them. Outside was gym equipment that Daniel had made, and when the students needed a recess, he would lead them in sports and games. Daniel's teaching methods were far ahead of his time.

Cecropia moth caterpillar, America's largest moth, was probably the type of worm Daniel received. He wrote that it was about the size of a man's middle finger, blue and gold, with black and gold horns running along its body and around its head. As a curious scientist, Daniel was determined to learn everything possible about this beautiful creature.

A good deed and the gift of a caterpillar helped to change Daniel's life. Daniel let a fatherless boy attend his school free of charge. The boy's sister was grateful and, knowing of Daniel's interest in science, she sent to school an unusual caterpillar she had found. Daniel could not identify the caterpillar, so he asked Dr. John Bachman, a famous naturalist and Lutheran minister, to identify it and keep it in his studio. Dr. Bachman agreed and invited Daniel to visit from time to time to watch the caterpillar's progress. They had long conversations while they explored Dr. Bachman's garden and his insect collection. Dr. Bachman was very impressed with Daniel's knowledge and his intelligence. A few years later, a letter from Dr. Bachman, full of Daniel's praises, opened the way for Daniel to go to college. Near the end of his life Daniel wrote that the hand of God must have been in that lowly worm.

Daniel's school flourished for about four years. Then one summer day in 1834, he sent three of his students to a nearby plantation to collect a live snake, a highland moccasin that Daniel had paid a slave on the plantation to catch for him. But before they could collect the snake, the boys ran into the plantation owner, Mr. Kennedy, and his son. They asked many questions about the things students were learning at Daniel's school. The Kennedys, who were important men in the area, were impressed with the answers, but they were not pleased. A school like Daniel's was a threat to slavery. His students might even gain more knowledge than the slaveholders!

That December a new law was passed in South Carolina. It would punish anyone who taught enslaved Blacks or free persons of color, or who kept a school for them. White persons would be fined $100 and sent to prison for six months. Free persons of color would be fined $50 and given fifty lashes with a whip. Enslaved persons would receive fifty lashes. The new law would take effect on April 1, 1835. Daniel decided to close his school. He would not risk being whipped and he could not afford the fine. He was heartbroken. He felt as if "some wild beast had plunged [its] fangs into [his] heart, and was squeezing out [his] life-blood." He even began to doubt God, but his doubt didn't last long. Calming himself by writing poetry, he poured out his feelings in a very long and sad farewell poem.

Once again Daniel was guided by a dream. This time he saw himself lifted up to the North, flying along the southern edges of the Great Lakes, wearing the pink robe—similar to a graduation gown—he always wore when he was teaching. He interpreted this to mean that he should go to a northern city, where he could teach without the restrictions he met in Charleston. Before he made his final decision, he sought the advice of some men he respected, including Dr. Bachman. They all agreed that he should go north, and they gave him letters that would introduce him to friends of theirs in New York and Philadelphia, important men who could help Daniel find work and get settled.

THE MOURNFUL LUTE, OR THE PRECEPTOR'S* FAREWELL

(Last three verses)

Pupils, attend my last departing sounds;
Ye are my hopes, and ye my mental crowns,
My monuments of intellectual might,
My robes of honor and my armor bright.
Like Solomon, entreat the throne of God;
Light shall descend in lucid columns broad,
And all that man has learned or man can know
In streams prolific shall your minds o'erflow.

Hate sin; love God; religion be your prize;
Her laws obeyed will surely make you wise,
Secure you from the ruin of the vain,
And save your souls from everlasting pain.
O fare you well for whom my bosom glows
With ardent love, which Christ my Savior knows!
For you I wept, and now for you I pray.

Farewell! Farewell! ye children of my love;
May joys abundant flow ye from above!
May peace celestial crown your useful days,
To bliss transported, sing eternal lays;
For sacred wisdom give a golden world,
And when foul vice his charming folds unfurl,
O spurn the monster, though his crystal eyes
Be like bright sunbeams streaming from the skies!
And I! O wither shall your tutor fly?
Guide thou my feet, great Sovereign of the sky.

A useful life by sacred wisdom crowned,
Is all I ask, let weal or woe abound!!

Daniel Alexander Payne, 1835

Poem written in grief after he felt forced to close his first school in Charleston.

* A preceptor is a teacher.

AM I NOT A MAN AND A BROTHER?

In July of 1835, a mob of citizens made a night time raid on the Charleston post office and ransacked the building (above). They tore open bundles of newspapers such as *The Liberator* and burned other abolitionist mail that they found. Note a sign reading "$20,000 Reward for Tappan" posted on the post office as bounty on the head of Arthur Tappan, founder and president of the American Anti-Slavery Society. The original caption read, "New method of assorting the mail, as practised by Southern slave-holders, or attack on the Post Office."

Am I not a Man and a Brother? (above left) was a popular image among abolitionists in England and the United States. Pro-slavery Southerners hated and feared this kind of material.

On the last week of school, Daniel invited the parents of his pupils and people in the community to come and see what the children had been learning. Daniel was proud of all that they had accomplished. "But the last month, the last week, the last day, and the last hour of this interesting school had come, and it closed as it had begun—with singing and prayer—on the last day of March, 1835." Many people were sorry to see Daniel leave Charleston, and many of them helped him with things he would need for the journey. When it was time to leave, a large group of friends came to the dock to see him off and wish him well. On Saturday, May 9, 1835, amid many tears, Daniel Alexander Payne boarded a steamboat headed for New York City.

Daniel A. Payne's signature.

THREE: 1835-1843
FIRST YEARS IN THE NORTH

"When God has a work to be executed he also chooses the man to execute it. He also qualifies the workman for the work . . . {t}he hour for the man and the man for the hour."
—Daniel A. Payne, *Recollections of Seventy Years*

SOON AFTER Daniel arrived in New York on May 13, he took his letters of introduction and went to meet the people to whom they were addressed. On his final visit Daniel presented his letter from Dr. Bachman to the Rev. Daniel Strobel, a Lutheran minister. Rev. Strobel had just learned that some students at a college in Pennsylvania wanted to give money to educate a talented, religious young man of color, who could then help the free people of color in this country. After reading Dr. Bachman's letter, Rev. Strobel was certain that Daniel was exactly the young man the students were looking for, and that God must have sent him right at that moment. He urged Daniel to go and attend the school, the Lutheran Theological Seminary at Gettysburg. A seminary is a school that trains ministers, and Daniel protested that he wanted to be a teacher, not a preacher. Rev. Strobel convinced Daniel that a college education would make him a better teacher, and that he would not have to become

Painting from life by A. Haffy. An inscription reads, "Rev. Daniel A. Payne, Minister of the African Methodist Episcopal Church."

a minister. Daniel became the first Black student at the seminary.

While at Gettysburg, Daniel spent many hours reading and studying. He earned money to help with his expenses by doing odd jobs such as cutting wood, shining shoes, and shaving people's beards. He also stayed busy in the community. He started a Sunday School for "colored" children in the neighborhood, and recruited seminary students and townspeople as volunteer teachers. He organized a self-improvement group for "colored" women. He also held religious meetings. At one of those meetings, he spoke for three straight hours, and lost his voice for three weeks. Daniel refused to join the Methodist Episcopal Church in Gettysburg, because its leaders were in favor of slavery. Instead he attached himself to a small Black church in Carlisle, a nearby town. Daniel soon became an active church leader. He helped in the Sunday School and often spoke from the pulpit. Once he walked 25 miles from Gettysburg to Carlisle to take some textbooks to a class he had organized.

Although Daniel was often homesick for Charleston, he was happy with his studies, his church and community work. But one day while he was lying in bed reading, he felt a sharp pain in his left eye, as if a needle was being stuck into his eyeball. He had strained his optic nerve, and the doctor's only advice was to rest and wear tinted glasses. It took an entire year for Daniel's eye to heal, and since he could not read during that time, he could not keep up with his studies. He had to leave the seminary after only two years. Even though he had not finished his program, however, he was still qualified to become a minister.

Soon after he dropped out of the seminary, Daniel felt the call to preach. He was lying in bed one day, thinking about his future, when he sensed a pressure, which he thought was coming from God. He believed that God was calling him to "preach the gospel." Dan-

WE ARE HERE AND ARE HERE TO STAY

WHEN DANIEL FIRST ARRIVED IN NEW YORK HE WAS URGED BY MANY OF THE PROMINENT WHITE MEN HE MET TO GO TO AFRICA RATHER THAN TO STAY IN THE UNITED STATES WHERE SLAVERY WAS STILL ENFORCED. DANIEL WAS OPPOSED TO THE IDEA, AND BEFORE HE WOULD ACCEPT A SCHOLARSHIP TO GETTYSBURG SEMINARY HE MADE SURE THAT THE LUTHERANS WHO WERE SPONSORING HIM WERE NOT PLANNING TO SEND HIM TO AFRICA AFTER HIS GRADUATION. THE SEMINARIANS AT GETTYSBURG WERE ABOLITIONISTS WHO WANTED TO HELP AFRICAN AMERICANS IN AMERICA. THE AMERICAN COLONIZATION SOCIETY (ACS) HAD BEEN FORMED IN 1817 IN ORDER TO SETTLE FREE BLACK AMERICANS IN AFRICA. MANY PROMINENT MEN BELONGED TO OR SUPPORTED THE GROUP, INCLUDING HENRY CLAY (MIDDLE LEFT), AND PRESIDENTS JAMES MADISON, JAMES MONROE AND THOMAS JEFFERSON. THE ACS RAISED MONEY BY SELLING LIFETIME MEMBERSHIPS IN THE SOCIETY FOR $30 EACH. MEMBERS RECEIVED A CERTIFICATE (BOTTOM LEFT) WITH A HENRY CLAY SIGNATURE. SOME BLACK LEADERS WERE ALSO IN FAVOR OF EMIGRATION BECAUSE THEY THOUGHT AFRICAN AMERICANS WOULD BE BETTER OFF IF THEY HAD THEIR OWN COUNTRY. FREDERICK DOUGLASS, HOWEVER, THE GREAT ABOLITIONIST AND ORATOR (TOP LEFT) WAS STRONGLY OPPOSED TO COLONIZATION AND SPOKE OUT AGAINST IT.

iel felt he had to answer the call. The Lutheran Church ordained him a minister, but they would not assign him to be the pastor of a Lutheran church. The president of the seminary, Dr. Schmucker, advised Daniel that he could be more helpful to people of color as a minister in a different denomination—the African Methodist Episcopal or AME (pronounced A-M-E) Church.

The AME Church had been organized many years earlier by Blacks protesting against discrimination in the Methodist Episcopal Church. Like other Black denominations, the AME Church was one of the few organizations that Black people controlled and operated, and it had thousands of members in the United States and in Canada. It was a network of individual churches located in many towns and cities; the church Daniel had attended in Carlisle was an

AME church. Local AME churches served their people in many ways, not just by holding religious services. They ran schools, fed the hungry, took care of the sick, and taught people how to improve their daily lives. Many local AME churches also served as stations on the Underground Railroad, helping escaped slaves to freedom. This was exactly the kind of denomination Daniel was looking for.

When Daniel left Gettysburg, he headed for Philadelphia, intending to join the AME Church. Along the way, however, he met a friend of

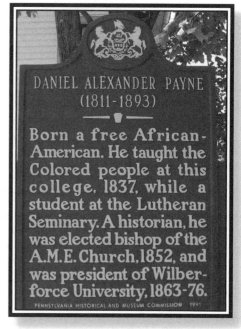

A marker on the campus of Gettysburg College honoring Daniel Payne.

DANIEL A. PAYNE

1906 photo of the AME church in Carlisle, PA, Daniel's church home when he was a student at Gettysburg Seminary.

his father's who told him that people in the AME Church did not want educated ministers. According to his story, AME preachers often boasted that they had not "rubbed their heads against college walls," or studied Latin, Greek, or Hebrew. The church members would approve, answering "Amen!" or " Glory to God!" This report was only partly true, but Daniel believed it, and since he was an educated minister, he was afraid he would not be welcome in the AME Church. He accepted an invitation to become the pastor of a "colored" Presbyterian church in East Troy, New York.

Daniel was just twenty-six years old, young and inexperienced. He was very eager to save souls, and at a New Year's Eve service in 1837, he preached too long and too loud, trying to touch people's hearts. Then after the service he prayed aloud for the rest of the night. As a result, he lost his voice for a whole year and had to

Bishop Morris Brown

carry around a slate and chalk so he could write down what he wanted to say. On top of that, he caught a terrible cold, which kept him in bed for four months. Because he could no longer carry out his duties, he resigned as pastor of the church at East Troy. Still a teacher at heart, Daniel moved to Philadelphia, and in early 1840 opened a school on Spruce Street. He started with only three students, but by the end of the year, all the students from the city's two other private schools for people of color had transferred to his school. Three years later the school had 60 students.

In Philadelphia, Daniel came into contact with some of the leading members of the AME Church, including Bishop Morris Brown, the senior AME bishop, and J. J. G. Bias, a prominent Black doctor who was involved with the Underground Railroad. In fact, Daniel became a member of a group called the Vigilance Committee, which helped about 300 runaway slaves a year get to safety. Bishop Brown and Dr. Bias urged Daniel to join the AME Church, and the more he learned about it, the more he wanted to be a part of it. Daniel became a member of Bethel AME Church, known as Mother Bethel, and he soon became the very first seminary-trained AME minister.

In 1843 Bishop Brown appointed Daniel to be the pastor of Israel AME Church in Washington, D.C. This appointment presented two problems. First, Daniel did not want to leave his school in Philadelphia. Second, he had promised himself when he left Charleston that he would never again live in a place where slavery was legal. He had seen how cruel slavery was, and had felt its sting even though he was legally free. Once in Charleston, a White man had knocked Daniel down because he was carrying a cane. The man thought a cane was too fancy for a Black man. Daniel had fought back and had gone to jail briefly. In 1843 slavery was still legal in Washington, D. C. Free people of color had to get permission to live in the city, and pay a $1000 bond to guarantee "good behavior." Daniel thought this was insulting, but after praying about his decision, he chose to pay the money and go to Washington because he thought it was his Christian duty.

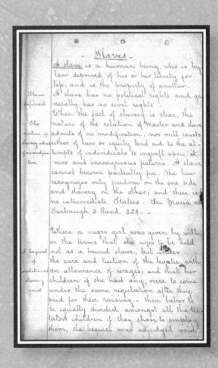

EVERY SLAVE STATE HAD SLAVE CODES LIKE THIS ONE FROM WASHINGTON, D.C. (RIGHT), DEFINING SLAVES AS PROPERTY. ABOLITIONIST SOJOURNER TRUTH (ABOVE) DEMANDED HUMANS RIGHTS FOR BLACK PEOPLE. HER LAWSUIT LED TO THE DESEGREGATION OF STREETCARS IN WASHINGTON, D.C.

"WE WISH TO PLEAD OUR OWN CAUSE"

WHEN DANIEL ARRIVED IN NEW YORK HE WAS IMMEDIATELY INTRODUCED TO SOME OF THE LEADING FREE BLACK CITIZENS AND ANTISLAVERY ACTIVISTS IN THE CITY. AMONG THOSE HE MET WERE THE REV. PETER WILLIAMS, JR. WHO WAS THE FIRST AFRICAN-AMERICAN ORDAINED EPISCOPAL PRIEST, AND LEWIS TAPPAN, CO-FOUNDER OF THE ANTISLAVERY SOCIETY. HE ALSO MET CHARLES B. RAY, EDITOR OF *THE COLORED AMERICAN* NEWSPAPER; CHARLES REASON, THE FIRST AFRICAN-AMERICAN PROFESSOR AT A WHITE COLLEGE AND PRINCIPAL OF ONE OF THE COUNTRY'S BEST AFRICAN-AMERICAN SCHOOLS, AND ALEXANDER CRUMMEL, WHO WOULD BECOME A FAMOUS EPISCOPAL PRIEST, AN EDUCATOR, AND A MISSIONARY TO LIBERIA. THESE MEN WERE HIGHLY RESPECTED FOR SPEAKING OUT AGAINST SLAVERY AND ON BEHALF OF THE RIGHTS OF AFRICAN AMERICANS. SOME OF THEM HAD AN IMPORTANT INFLUENCE ON DANIEL'S THINKING. MOREOVER, THEY CONNECTED HIM TO A COMMUNITY OF ACTIVISTS WHOSE IMPACT WAS FELT NATIONALLY AND BEYOND.

Rev. Peter Williams, Jr.

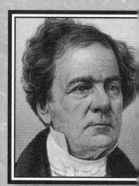

Lewis Tappan

Rev. Charles B. Ray

Charles L. Reason

Alexander Crummell

Rev. Samuel Cornish

John Brown Russwurm

ALSO AMONG THE NEW YORKERS DANIEL MET WERE THE
REV. SAMUEL CORNISH AND JOHN BROWN RUSSWURM,
CO-EDITORS OF *FREEDOM'S JOURNAL* (BELOW), THE
FIRST NEWSPAPER OWNED AND OPERATED BY AFRICAN
AMERICANS. MANY OF THESE LEADERS WOULD PROBABLY
HAVE BEEN INVOLVED IN BLACK CONVENTIONS LIKE THE ONE
IN WASHINGTON, D.C. (ABOVE), WHERE DELEGATES SOUGHT
WAYS TO HELP THE PEOPLE IN THEIR COMMUNITIES.

FOUR: 1843-1852
THE RISE TO LEADERSHIP

"He was a child of the church, and in time became its father."
—Frederick Douglass, Remarks on Bishop Daniel A. Payne
The Frederick Douglass Papers at the Library of Congress

WHEN DANIEL arrived at Israel AME Church he found a huge building with no seats on the lower level. He set to work with some carpenter's tools, and in a few weeks he had "fully seated" the church. That done, he turned his attention to the people. He set up a scientific and literary class in the church, and started the nation's first organization of Black pastors. He also launched a campaign to require that AME ministers had to be educated.

Very few AME ministers at the time had had an opportunity to get an advanced education. Some had very little education at all. Daniel was wise enough to know that if the AME Church was to continue to thrive and grow, its ministers needed to be educated. They needed to be able to understand and carry out the laws of the Church, manage Church affairs, interpret the Bible clearly, and teach their members how to live as good Christians. He also knew

that, unless ministers were educated, they would not be able to keep up with younger church members, who would have greater educational opportunities than their elders had.

As Daniel had heard, many AME ministers at the time were content to be uneducated. They and some of their members believed that all they needed was to be inspired or called by God; they thought education might even make them feel farther away from God. Others agreed with Daniel, including Bishop Morris Brown, who had very little schooling himself, but was highly respected for his wisdom and his leadership. Ministers and church members lined up on both sides of the issue; change would not come without a fight.

Daniel's main weapon in this battle was his pen. He wrote five long letters, or epistles, which he published in the AME Church magazine. His letters urged AME ministers to take every opportunity to educate themselves. He also argued that anyone who wanted to be an AME minister should be required to study certain subjects, including English grammar, arithmetic, geography, history, and theology or religious studies. A tide of angry letters arrived at the magazine, accusing Daniel of insulting AME ministers and doing the devil's work. Only a few took Daniel's side.

If Daniel was to win this battle, Church officials would have to vote in favor of his idea at an AME General Conference, a meeting held every four years. A General Conference was to be held in Pittsburgh in 1844, but Daniel was so upset about the ugly things his enemies had said and written that he decided not to attend. Bishop Brown persuaded him to change his mind. Daniel went to the conference and presented his resolution—to require ministers to study certain subjects—but he did not explain why it was a good idea because he thought most of the church leaders at the conference already agreed with him. He was wrong; the resolution was overwhelmingly defeated. There was such uproar over the vote that Daniel must have felt as if he had been thrown into a lion's den, like his namesake in the Bible, the prophet Daniel.

Just as an angel kept the lions from eating the prophet, Rev. Abram Lewis kept the delegates from defeating Daniel's resolution. The next morning, Rev. Lewis asked the delegates to reconsider. He then made a passionate speech in favor of the resolution. He argued that as leaders, the delegates had a duty to pave the way for the next generation. Rev. Lewis' speech was so convincing that even before he could finish, the delegates started shouting, "Give us

First released in 1817, The Doctrines and Discipline of the AME Church *is one of the first books published by African Americans. It is updated every four years.*

the resolution! Give us the resolution." Then every delegate voted "yes" and Daniel's resolution became a part of the Discipline—the rules—of the AME Church. From then on, anyone who wanted to be an AME minister had to study the subjects Daniel had outlined in his letters. After the conference, he published eight more essays explaining and defending the new rules.

"THIS FAR BY FAITH"

Top left: *Family worship on a South Carolina plantation.* Top right: *Pew and pulpit in a slave cabin.* Center: *An 1804 engraving of Mother Bethel AME Church, Philadelphia. This structure replaced the renovated blacksmith shop that was dedicated in 1794 and served as the congregation's first place of worship.* Lower left: *Baptist Church in Savannah, GA, founded in 1788. One of the first independent Black churches.* Lower right: *Richard Allen, founder and first bishop of the African Methodist Episcopal Church.*

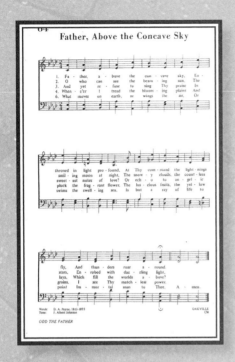

Top: Hymn from the current AME Hymnal, with words by Daniel A. Payne, showing his idea of proper worship. Bottom: Ring shout, Simons Island, GA. Worshippers danced, clapped and sang to convert sinners. Payne called the rings heathenish and disgraceful.

MANY AFRICAN AMERICANS BECAME CHRISTIANS EARLY IN AMERICAN HISTORY. IN THE PLANTATION SOUTH, SLAVEHOLDERS TRIED TO CONTROL AFRICAN-AMERICAN WORSHIP AND THE BIBLE LESSONS SLAVES RECEIVED. SLAVEHOLDERS HELD AND ATTENDED WORSHIP SERVICES SET UP ON THEIR PLANTATIONS FOR THEIR FAMILIES AND THEIR SLAVES. ENSLAVED AFRICAN AMERICANS, HOWEVER, OFTEN WORSHIPPED ON THEIR OWN IN SECRET. EVENTUALLY, AFRICAN AMERICANS IN THE NORTH AND SOUTH BEGAN TO BREAK AWAY FROM WHITE-CONTROLLED CHURCHES, WHERE THEY OFTEN MET DISCRIMINATION. ONE OF THE FIRST BLACK BAPTIST CHURCHES WAS FORMED IN SAVANNAH, GEORGIA IN 1788. IN 1787, RICHARD ALLEN, A PHILADELPHIA METHODIST MINISTER AND FORMER SLAVE, LED A GROUP OF BLACK WORSHIPPERS TO FORM WHAT BECAME THE AFRICAN METHODIST EPISCOPAL CHURCH. AFRICAN-AMERICAN CHURCHES DEVELOPED VARIOUS FORMS OF WORSHIP, SOME OF WHICH, LIKE THE RING SHOUTS, RETAINED THE SPIRIT OF AFRICAN EXPRESSIONS. OTHERS STAYED CLOSE TO THE WORSHIP TRADITIONS AND ORGANIZATIONAL STRUCTURES OF THE PROTESTANT CHURCHES FROM WHICH THEY HAD BROKEN AWAY.

At the same General Conference, Daniel also introduced a number of other resolutions that changed or established new policies for the AME Church, or improved its organization. The only person who was more active than Daniel at that conference was Bishop Brown, who was in charge. Later, Daniel would write that the 1844 General Conference was the start of a new chapter in the history of the AME Church. It also marked a new chapter in his own life. He was only 33 years old. He had been in the AME Church just three years; yet he had become one of its best-known and most influential leaders.

In 1845 Daniel was assigned to Bethel AME Church in Baltimore, Maryland. There he opened the last elementary school he would operate himself. Like the others, the school was highly successful; within one year his school grew from three students to 50. While he was pastor at Bethel Baltimore, he also oversaw the building of a magnificent new church building. To raise money for the new building, Daniel presented a concert of sacred music. He hired James Fleet, the best Black musician in Washington, D.C., to put together a group of singers and musicians who played the flute, the guitar, the piano, and a large stringed instrument called the bass viol. Daniel wanted to be certain that all of the words, or lyrics, of the songs would be appropriate for church, so he wrote all the lyrics himself, and had them set to music. The concert was so successful that Daniel arranged for a second concert, featuring seven violins and a singer.

These were the first times that instrumental music had been played in an AME church. Thanks to Daniel's leadership, before long every AME Church wanted musical instruments. A few years earlier, Daniel had helped to introduce choir singing into the AME Church. When a few talented singers had formed a choir at Mother

Bethel in Philadelphia, some members were so unhappy they left the church for good. They had been used to everybody singing together, with one person leading. They thought a choir was the work of the devil. Daniel preached a special sermon that helped the people understand why sacred choir music was suitable for church services. They began to accept choir singing, and choirs soon became a normal part of AME churches.

Daniel also tried to change or do away with some forms of worship that he thought were not proper. He was especially unhappy about "Praying and Singing Bands," in which people would form a circle and clap their hands, stamp their feet and sing loudly. Usually these

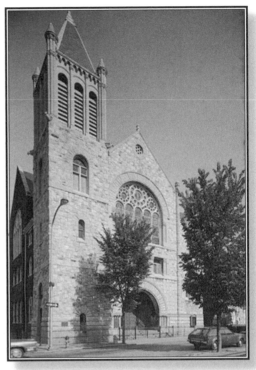

Bethel AME Church, Philadelphia, in 1973. "Mother Bethel," the first AME church. The fourth building on this site, it was dedicated by Daniel Payne in 1890.

circles or rings would form after a church service, and last until late at night. It was the way the people expressed their religious spirit. He called the rings ridiculous and disgusting, especially because some of their songs were not the kind he thought appropriate for church. He called them "cornfield ditties," and gave an example in his journal:

> *Ashes to ashes, dust to dust*
> *If God won't have us, the devil must.*

This way of worshipping was very popular in many AME churches, and it took some courage to try to stop it. Daniel seldom lacked courage when he thought he was doing the right thing. He thought the Bible called for worship that was more quiet and reserved, so he discouraged the rings, and tried to stop them whenever he could. This battle went on for years, not just in Baltimore, but in many AME churches.

In 1847, when he was 36, Daniel married Mrs. Julia Farris, a widow from Washington, D.C. Less than a year later she gave birth to their daughter, who was named Julia Ann after her mother. Sadly, Daniel's wife died just a few hours after the baby was born. Daniel was heartbroken. He poured out his grief in a long poem, which he called "My Julia." But even more heartbreak was to come. Baby Julia Ann died when she was just nine months old. Once again Daniel turned to poetry to express his deep sadness. He took some comfort in his belief that his wife and daughter were with God.

While he was grieving the loss of his wife and baby, he also had to struggle with a small group of officers who tried to take over running Bethel Church. They did not succeed, but the conflict caused Daniel much distress. In 1848 he had been chosen to write the history of the AME Church, and early in 1850, he decided it was time to start working on that project. Daniel asked Bishop William Paul Quinn not to assign him to a church so he could work full time on the history project. The bishop refused this request, but he did assign Daniel to little Ebenezer AME Church in Baltimore, thinking that a smaller church would leave Daniel some time to work on the history.

When Daniel arrived at Ebenezer, however, he was met by a group of church officers who told him that the people of that church did not want him as their pastor. They said they knew he was a good person, but they thought he was too proud, he had too fine a carpet on his floor, he wouldn't have tea with the members, and he wouldn't let them sing their spiritual songs. Their charges were untrue (except the one about the songs) and Daniel thought they were unfair. He said to the officers, "Goodbye, brothers, I shall never cross your threshold again as your pastor." In a way, he was relieved, because he was now free to gather the information he needed to write the history of the AME Church.

For the next two years, 1850 to 1852, Daniel traveled to every AME church he could reach. He visited churches from Maryland to Maine, from New Jersey to Missouri, and as far south as New Orleans. He also visited all the AME churches in Canada. He collected all the written records he could find from each church—minutes of church meetings, pamphlets, programs, even scraps of paper people had written on. He read the journals of early AME Church leaders,

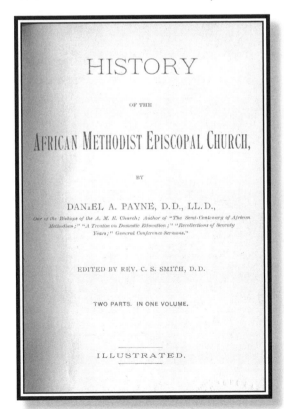

Title page of Daniel Payne's History of the African Methodist Episcopal Church, *published in 1891.*

WHO IS SUFFICIENT?

ALTHOUGH DANIEL PAYNE WAS NOT CERTAIN HE WAS PREPARED FOR THE POSITION, HE BECAME ONE OF THE AME CHURCH'S MOST HIGHLY ACCLAIMED BISHOPS. THIS STAINED GLASS WINDOW HONORING HIS LEGACY IS IN THE CHAPEL AT PAYNE THEOLOGICAL SEMINARY. IT SHOWS A BIBLE IN HIS HAND AND THE ORIGINAL BUILDING OF WILBERFORCE UNIVERSITY ABOVE HIS HEAD. AT THE BOTTOM IS THE OFFICIAL MOTTO OF THE AME CHURCH, "GOD OUR FATHER, CHRIST OUR REDEEMER, MAN OUR BROTHER."

The Episcopal (bishop's) Seal of the AME Church, with the Church motto, was created under the supervision of Daniel A. Payne.

DANIEL A. PAYNE

especially the "father" and first Bishop of the AME Church, Richard Allen. He interviewed people who had known Richard Allen or who had participated in early AME Church meetings. Without Daniel's efforts, much of the early history of the AME Church might have been lost. Daniel had taught himself how to be a historian, but he did the job so well that even today anyone who wants to know the early history of the AME Church must read Daniel's book.

Daniel's last stop in his travels was New York City, to attend the 1852 AME General Conference. He had traveled so much he had nearly worn out his clothes; he even called himself the "shabbiest member of the conference." Nevertheless, Bishop Quinn ordered Daniel to deliver the opening sermon. Daniel had just two hours to prepare, but he delivered what some people think was his very best sermon. It was based on the Bible verse, "Who Is Sufficient for These Things?" (*II Corinthians, 2:16*). He preached about the duties of a minister, and about the qualities and characteristics a minister should have. His main point was that in all things a minister must model himself after Jesus Christ.

The most important business at the conference was to elect two new bishops. Daniel was one of four candidates. When the election results were announced and Daniel learned that he was to be a bishop, he "trembled from head to foot and wept." He was afraid he didn't have the physical strength, or the necessary knowledge to be a bishop. Furthermore even though he had tried all his life to model himself after Jesus, just as he had urged others to do in his sermon, he thought he still wasn't righteous enough for such a "high, holy, and responsible position." Nevertheless, on May 13, 1852, Daniel Alexander Payne was consecrated the sixth bishop of the African Methodist Episcopal Church, the highest office in the Church.

The first eleven bishops of the AME Church, with the founder, Bishop Richard Allen, in the center. Daniel A. Payne is positioned at about 2 o'clock. These pioneers were very influential in the growth of the AME Church. The side images depict some important Church history and activities, including its book depository, two Church schools, and its first missionaries to Haiti.

FIVE: 1852-1863
A BATTLING BISHOP

"His firmness of character was his fortress
and his good conscience his defense."
—Benjamin F. Lee, *The AME Review*, July 1911

THE WORD "bishop" means "overseer" or "superinten-
dent," and for the next 41 years, Bishop Daniel Payne was one
of the most important overseers of the AME Church. Daniel was
a mite of a man, not more than five feet tall, thin and bony, and
he never in his life weighed more than 100 pounds, but he was a
mighty warrior for the AME Church and for Black people. One of
his main battles was for education. He believed the AME Church
needed not only educated ministers, but also educated members.
Wherever he went he either started or encouraged schools, Sunday Schools, study groups for ministers, and improvement societies for women. He also published poems, essays, and articles that
he thought would encourage Church members and others. He
thought Black people should be knowledgeable about many subjects, and he led the AME Church to publish a literary magazine,

which he edited for a while, and which lasted about seven years.

Soon after he was elected bishop, Daniel set out to oversee the churches in his district. He usually stayed in the homes of church members because in his day most hotels would not welcome Black guests. Most church members considered it an honor to have a bishop as a guest in their home, but Daniel often would not tell people who he was. He did not want to receive special treatment just because he was a bishop. Once, in a small town in Pennsylvania, a couple wouldn't let him into their house, only to discover when they went to church the next day that they had turned away the bishop. That day he preached a sermon about Christians' duty to be kind to one another, to be welcoming even to strangers, and not to judge people by their appearance. The couple was so embarrassed that even Daniel felt sorry for them. But he never hesitated to let people know when he thought they were not following the teachings of the Bible.

Daniel tried his best to live by his religious beliefs, and he expected other people to do the same. He thought that drinking alcohol and smoking tobacco were sinful, and he established or actively encouraged Temperance Societies, or anti-alcohol groups, among church members. One story says that at a conference banquet Daniel swept

Page from the history of Bethel AME Church, Pottsville, PA, describing Payne's visit.

DANIEL A. PAYNE

all the bottles of wine off the long dinner table and threw them out the door as far as he could. Rules were important too. Another story says that when a distinguished visitor put his hat on a chair in Daniel's home, Daniel sat on the hat, and when it was time to leave, he gave the visitor back his crumpled hat, along with money for a new one. Daniel believed that hats should be placed on hat racks, not chairs.

Many of his battles were church battles. Soon after he became bishop, a White woman became a member of Mother Bethel. Many of the women members did not want her in their church, even though she was running a school for Black children. No doubt the women of Mother Bethel had been treated badly by White people who believed Black people were inferior. They were probably afraid this woman would look down on them, too. They demanded that the pastor expel her from the church, and he reluctantly carried out their wishes. At the next annual conference, Daniel refused to appoint the pastor to a church, saying, "The pastor who would turn away from God's sanctuary any human being on account of color was not fit to have charge of a gang of dogs." The pastor went to see Daniel, and angrily shook his fist in Daniel's face saying, "You dare to leave me without an appointment because of that White woman! Open your mouth, if you dare, and I will lay you flat upon the floor." Daniel simply remained calm and quiet, and after a few minutes, the pastor turned around and left. Another bishop, with Daniel's permission, assigned him to a church in Canada.

More often, Daniel had to fight prejudice and discrimination against himself. For the first two-thirds of his life, slavery was legal in the United States, and Black people all over the country were often deprived of their rights. On several occasions, Daniel was mistreated on trains or ships because he was Black, even though he paid as much for his ticket as everybody else. He was also not free to travel everywhere in the country. In 1856, he had to go to St. Louis, Missouri on church business. Missouri was a slave state, and it was against the law for him to come into the state to preach. Daniel was arrested, but a lawyer was able to get him released because officials had put the wrong name, Thomas Payne, on the legal papers. The lawyer warned Daniel's friend, Rev. Jordan Early, to whisk Daniel out of town before the officials could correct their mistake. Just as they were leaving in Jordan Early's carriage, an official arrived waving legal papers and shouting, "Stop that horse! Stop that horse!" But Rev. Early sped away and didn't stop until they were across the Mississippi River and in free territory in Illinois. In time the case was dismissed.

On April 14, 1862, Daniel took his fight against slavery directly to the President of the United States. On that day he went to the White House to talk to President Abraham Lincoln. Congress had voted to abolish slavery in Washington, D.C., and Daniel wanted to urge the President to sign the bill into law. It must have been a sight—the short, slightly built bishop, shaking hands with the very tall and lanky President. Congressman Washburn and General Shurz were also in the room at the time. Daniel spoke right up. He said to Lincoln, "I am here to learn whether or not you intend to sign the bill of emancipation." The President did not give a direct answer. He noted that some people had come that day to ask him not to sign. The general spoke in favor of the bill. Daniel told Lincoln that the "colored" people had been praying for him, as the President had asked the nation to do. Lincoln seemed pleased to hear that news, but he still would not give a yes or no answer. After

THE SLOW DEATH OF SLAVERY

Legal slavery died a very slow death. In 1846 Dred Scott, (above) a Missouri slave who had lived in free territory, sued for his freedom. In 1857 the Supreme Court ruled against him, saying that Black people could not be citizens. Five years later, even as Abraham Lincoln prepared to free slaves in rebel states, he stated in a letter to editor Horace Greeley (right) that his actual goal was to save the Union.

THE UNION AND SLAVERY.

Letter From the President to Horace Greeley

EXECUTIVE MANSION,
WASHINGTON, Aug. 22, 1862.

Hon. Horace Greeley:

DEAR SIR: I have just read yours of the 19th, addressed to myself through the New-York *Tribune*. If there be in it any statements or assumptions of fact which I may know to be erroneous, I do not now and here controvert them. If there be in it any inference which I may believe to be falsely drawn, I do not now and here argue against them. If there be perceptible in it an impatient and dictatorial tone, I waive it in deference to an old friend, whose heart I have always supposed to be right.

As to the policy I "seem to be pursuing," as you say, I have not meant to leave any one in doubt.

I would save the Union. I would save it the shortest way under the Constitution. The sooner the national authority can be restored the nearer the Union will be "the Union as it was." If there be those who would not save the Union unless they could at the same time *save* Slavery, I do not agree with them. If there be those who would not save the Union unless they could at the same time *destroy* Slavery, I do not agree with them. My paramount object in this struggle *is* to save the Union, and is *not* either to save or destroy Slavery. If I could save the Union without freeing any slave, I would do it, and if I could save it by freeing all the slaves, I would do it, and if I could save it by freeing some and leaving others alone, I would also do that. What I do about Slavery and the colored race, I do because I believe it helps to save this Union, and what I forbear, I forbear because I do *not* believe it would help to save the Union. I shall do *less* whenever I shall believe what I am doing hurts the cause, and I shall do *more* whenever I shall believe doing more will help the cause. I shall try to correct errors when shown to be errors; and I shall adopt new views so fast as they shall appear to be true views. I have here stated my purpose according to my view of *official* duty, and I intend no modification of my oft-expressed *personal* wish that all men, everywhere, could be free. Yours,

A. LINCOLN.

President Abraham Lincoln

about 45 minutes, Daniel thought he should leave. He gave the President an AME newspaper and magazine so he could read about the progress of the AME Church. Two days later, on April 16, 1862, Abraham Lincoln signed the bill, and slavery was finally outlawed in the nation's capital.

By that time Daniel was living in Ohio. In the summer of 1854, he married Mrs. Eliza Clark, a widow with four children. Three were at home—Laura, who was eighteen; John, who was sixteen; and Augusta, who was six. Eliza also had an older stepson, Peter Clark. They lived in Cincinnati for a while, but Daniel thought the city was a terrible place to raise children; it was full of "corrupting influences." He searched for a place where the two younger children could go to school, and settled on a location near Xenia, Ohio, named Tawawa Springs, now called Wilberforce. It was on the grounds of what had once been a fancy resort hotel, with a large main building and several cottages. In July 1856, Daniel and his family happily moved into one of the smaller homes, which they named Evergreen Cottage. For the Payne family, the thick green grass and many trees were a welcome change; even their pet dog enjoyed the new surroundings. Evergreen Cottage would become Daniel's permanent home. Not surprisingly, one of the first things Daniel did was to organize a church in his home. He named it Zion's Chapel, and at first there were just four members. Later it was moved out of the cottage and became the Holy Trinity AME Church, which still exists.

The Cincinnati Conference of the Methodist Episcopal Church had bought the hotel and its grounds to use as a school for the education of "colored" people. The Methodists called the school a university, even though at the time it was more like an elementary and high school. They named the school after William Wilber-

The original buildings of Wilberforce University, c. 1856.

force, a famous British abolitionist who had fought fiercely against slavery in his country. Wilberforce University opened in October 1856, with M. M. P. Gaddis as its principal. There was also a Board of Trustees, a group of men who were responsible for watching over the school and managing its affairs. Four of the 24 Board members were "men of color." Daniel was the most active of the four. He lived on campus, he was a member of the Executive Committee, and in the summer, he was in charge of the school.

Most of the first students at Wilber-

Daniel A. Payne and his second wife Eliza Clark Payne, c. 1854.

force were from the South, the sons and daughters of slaveholding planters and enslaved women. There were no colleges and very few schools of any kind that those children could attend in the South, so their fathers sent them to Ohio to be educated. Then in 1861, the Civil War broke out, and most of the Southern slaveholders took their children out of school. With too few students and too little money, Wilberforce could not continue to operate. The Methodist Church closed the school in 1862. Early the next year, the university President, Dr. Richard Rust, informed Daniel that if the AME Church wanted to buy Wilberforce, they could have it for $10,000, which was the amount the Methodists still owed.

On March 10, 1863, Daniel was called to Cincinnati for a special meeting of the Wilberforce trustees. The State of Ohio wanted to buy the property, and they were willing to pay much more than $10,000. The trustees urged Daniel to buy the school for the AME Church. Daniel had sought advice from AME Church leaders, but he did not yet have permission to buy the school. Daniel said he needed three more months. The trustees said, "Now or never." It was after 9 p.m.; the state needed an answer by 11 o'clock the next morning. Daniel did not have even ten dollars in his pocket, let alone ten thousand dollars. But he stepped out on faith and declared, "In the name of the Lord I buy the property of Wilberforce for the African Methodist Episcopal Church."

By June, Daniel and his supporters had raised $2500 dollars for the first payment, and on June 11, 1863, the school was officially turned over to Daniel Alexander Payne, James A. Shorter and John G. Mitchell, as agents for the AME Church. With that, Wilberforce University became the first college in the United States owned and operated by Blacks. Daniel was elected president, making him the first Black president of an African-American college.

THE CIVIL WAR

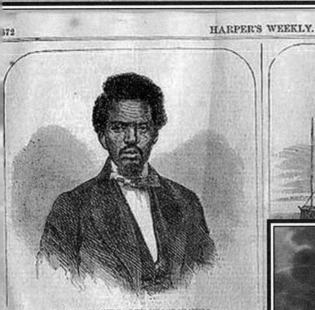

HARPER'S WEEKLY. [June 14, 1862.

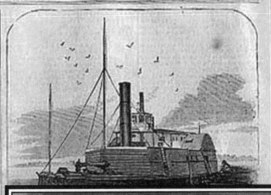

THE STEAMER "PLANTER" AND HER CAPTOR.

WHEN ABRAHAM LINCOLN WAS ELECTED PRESIDENT IN 1860, DANIEL'S HOME STATE, SOUTH CAROLINA, WAS THE FIRST TO SECEDE FROM THE UNITED STATES. SOUTH CAROLINA AND OTHER SOUTHERN STATES FORMED A REBEL CONFEDERATE GOVERNMENT AND ON APRIL 12, 1861, REBELS STARTED THE CIVIL WAR BY FIRING ON FORT SUMTER IN CHARLESTON HARBOR. IN MAY 1862 ROBERT SMALLS, (ABOVE LEFT) AN ENSLAVED SHIP'S PILOT, DARINGLY STOLE THE CONFEDERATE SHIP "PLANTER" OUT OF CHARLESTON HARBOR PAST FORT SUMTER (SHOWN ABOVE), AND TURNED IT OVER TO THE UNION.

WILBERFORCE UNIVERSITY, XENIA, OHIO.

Wilberforce University Campus, as it looked in the 1850s.

THE "FATHER" OF WILBERFORCE UNIVERSITY

"He carried the torchlight of education everywhere he went."
—Frederick Douglass, Remarks on Bishop Daniel A. Payne
The Frederick Douglass Papers at the Library of Congress

WILBERFORCE UNIVERSITY opened as an AME school on July 3, 1863 with six students studying elementary subjects. John G. Mitchell was principal and teacher; his wife, Fannie B. Mitchell, was his assistant. By the spring of 1864, they had enough students to hire a second teacher, Mrs. Esther Maltby. For the first two years, Wilberforce continued to grow while Daniel and John Mitchell raised money to pay off the school's debt. Just when they had raised all except the last payment of $2500, tragedy struck.

On April 14, 1865—the same day Abraham Lincoln was shot and killed—someone set fire to the main building at Wilberforce and burned it to the ground. Fortunately, almost all the students had gone to Xenia to attend a celebration of the end of the Civil War. Daniel was holding a conference in Baltimore; Mr. Mitchell was with the students. Mrs. Maltby was the only adult on campus.

She refused to shut down the school. She turned one of the cottages into a classroom and classes continued until the school year ended. When Daniel returned to the campus in June, his heart ached when he saw the ruins of the building, but he declared, "From these ashes a nobler building shall arise!" Before he resigned as president eleven years later, he made sure this prediction came true.

While he was president of Wilberforce, Daniel was also still a bishop. Some people thought he should give up one of those jobs, but he loved them both too much to even think of doing that. After the Baltimore Conference, he took a steam ship from New York to his home city, Charleston, arriving exactly thirty years after he had left to go North. Daniel was overjoyed to meet old friends and schoolmates, but saddened by all the destruction left by the war. He visited "colored" schools, and was delighted to learn that there were about 3000 "colored" children going to school in Charleston. His main work, though, was to organize a group of southern churches into the South Carolina Conference of the AME Church.

During the time slavery was legal, the AME Church had been outlawed in most of the South, including South Carolina, because slaveholders rightly suspected it was an "abolition church." Once the Civil War was over, thousands of free and newly freed Black people were hungry for the religious services and the education that they had been denied. The AME Church, along with other organizations, was very much involved in establishing new churches and setting up schools. Although Daniel's work at Wilberforce meant that he couldn't travel very much, he did everything he could. He established new churches, he urged the AME Church to send missionaries to the South, he raised money to support the schools and the churches and, as often as possible, he sent preachers from the North to the South to help.

CELEBRATION OF THE ABOLITION OF SLAVERY IN THE DISTRICT OF COLUMBIA BY THE COLORED PEOPLE, IN WASHINGTON, April 19, 1866.—[SKETCHED BY F. DIELMAN.]

Free African Americans celebrating the fourth anniversary of the abolition of slavery in Washington, DC, which occurred in April 1862.

It was at the end of his homecoming trip to Charleston, in June of 1865, that Daniel returned to Wilberforce to find the building in ashes. Determined to keep the school going, he threw himself into the work of the university. He was truly "The Father of Wilberforce," involved in every part of campus life. He hired teachers, he taught classes, he raised money, he recruited promising students, and he enforced the school rules. One of his students, Hallie Quinn Brown, wrote about her memories of Wilberforce and President Payne. He was known on campus for keeping strict hours—getting up every morning at 4 a.m. and going to bed at 9 p.m. He would leave any event, no matter how important, so he could get to bed by 9 p.m.. He was also very careful with his diet. He ate very little meat and drank uncolored tea. Miss Brown wrote that in winter he sometimes looked like a chubby little person, because he wore so many clothes—heavy wool underwear and socks, two or three coats, thick boots, and a wide-brimmed hat.

Hallie Quinn Brown also remembered Mrs. Eliza Payne as being an important part of campus life and a big help to her husband. Unlike Daniel, she was "tall and stately," as well as stylish. On special occasions she wore "elegant black silks, fine crepe shawls and elaborate fringes. Her dresses were long and swept the floor. ... She was graceful as a swan." She was the "First Lady" of Wilberforce. As college president and bishop, Daniel had many important visitors, and it was Eliza's job to welcome them and treat them as special guests. Hallie Brown reported that "Ma Payne" as the students called her, made Evergreen Cottage a warm and pleasant place for visitors of all kinds, ministers and strangers alike.

Students thought Daniel was kind and fatherly, but that he was also very strict. As a teacher, he expected great things from his students, and would not put up with sloppy work. Sometimes he did show a bit of humor, although it might have had a bite to it. An older student named McClung was having trouble with a subject Daniel was teaching. After a few days of unsuccessfully trying to help the student understand, Daniel said to the students, "I advised the class, a short time ago, to eat fish, which is said to be a good brain food. I advise Brother McClung to eat a whale."

Under Daniel's leadership, Wilberforce had plenty of rules, and before a student was admitted he or she had to agree to follow every one of them. Students had to attend chapel every morning, with their bibles in hand. They had to go to church and Sunday School every

Sunday. One rule even said they had to take a bath on Saturday night. Students could not smoke cigarettes or drink beer or wine. If they were caught smoking or drinking alcohol, they would be sent home. Students had to keep their rooms clean and the classrooms neat and in order; faculty could visit students' rooms at any time. And when it was study time, students had to be studying. A Wilberforce student was expected not only to learn school subjects, but also to behave the way their teachers thought a good Christian should.

Daniel also worked hard to turn the school from what was basically an elementary and high school

Hallie Quinn Brown—teacher, author, elocutionist, activist.

into a real university. Within three years they were offering college courses. Daniel urged every large AME church to send at least one student to Wilberforce and pay his or her expenses, which amounted to about $150 for a year. He hired the best professors he could find, and was proud that Wilberforce did not exclude anyone—not students, or professors, or trustees—because of the color of their skin. Most colleges in the United States at the time would not accept Blacks as students or teachers. Among the Wilberforce professors were men and women, Black and White Americans, and people from countries such as England and Scotland. By the time Daniel resigned as president, Wilberforce had graduated 29 students with college degrees—13 women and 16 men. All of them had become either ministers or teachers.

Much of Daniel's time as president was spent trying to raise money to keep the college going. In his travels he had met many famous or wealthy people, and he himself had become well known. Although it was not always easy, he was able to get contributions from some of those people and from some government organizations. In 1867, Daniel took his first trip to Europe, to raise money for Wilberforce and attend a church meeting in Amsterdam. He also hoped to find some new teachers for the university. He spent a year in Europe, visiting in London, Amsterdam and Paris. He saw some famous places, met and made friends with some important people, and preached and gave several speeches. But he was not successful either in raising money or finding teachers. Even the son of William Wilberforce, the man the school was named for, would not give money for the college. Daniel returned home disappointed, but not defeated. He continued to try to raise money and to keep Wilberforce growing and improving. Even after he was no longer president, Daniel continued to work for the benefit of Wilberforce. He asked for and received money from a friend, the Unitarian minister John Ware, to buy materials for an art room, which Daniel called the Ware Art Room. Daniel thought Wilberforce should also have a science museum. A professor offered to sell Daniel his museum, which was worth $2000, at a bargain price of $1400. But the Wilberforce Board of Trustees "wouldn't touch it with a forty-foot pole." Daniel had to raise the money by himself, and ended up spending more than $300 of his own money. When it opened, it was fittingly named the Payne Museum.

The 1868 AME General Conference, Washington, D.C. Bishop Daniel Payne is seated in the center of the first row.

In 1873, Bishop Quinn died, and Daniel became the senior bishop of the AME Church. In 1876, he turned 65. At the General Conference in Atlanta that year, he resigned as president of Wilberforce. He had been its most important guiding force, almost single-handedly keeping the school going. He had kept his promise to construct a "nobler" building to replace the one that had been burned. The old building had been made of wood; the new one was red brick. It was a huge U-shaped building, three stories tall, with a basement. It included nine classrooms, an art room, a music room, and a space for a museum. It also had forty bedrooms, for eighty students. In the basement were a kitchen, a dining hall, storerooms, a laundry, and sleeping rooms for the staff. The school was out of debt, and was worth about $60,000. Six classes had graduated, and the school had a fine, well-educated faculty. Daniel was pleased to report that its faculty and trustees included not just AMEs, but Methodists, Baptists, Presbyterians, Congregationalists, Unitarians, Quakers, and Catholics. When he turned Wilberforce over to its next president, Benjamin F. Lee, it was in fine condition.

THE FINAL YEARS

"A Useful Life by Holy Wisdom Crowned."
—Daniel A. Payne, "the Mournful Lute," in *Recollections of Seventy Years*

ONE REASON Daniel resigned as president of Wilberforce was so he could write. He needed to finish writing the history of the AME Church, and he was working on a book about his own life. He had also been working on a book about domestic education—how and what parents should teach their children at home. He had become an expert by studying everything he could find by experts on childhood education. In his book Daniel recommended that parents educate themselves, and suggested some books for them to read. He also listed the subjects parents should teach their children. He even included songs that he had written to be used for family religious services at home. He thought mothers had a special responsibility to bring up their children as intelligent Christians with good character. He urged them to teach their children from the beginning to "value learning more than silver and wisdom more than gold." His main theme was from the Bible: "Train up a child in the way he should go, and when he is old he will not depart from it." (*Proverbs 22:6*) Daniel believed very strongly that Christian education was necessary for the AME Church, for all Black people, and for the nation.

Sometime in the early 1880s, Daniel started spending winters in Jacksonville, Florida, to avoid the cold winters in Ohio, but his main home was still Evergreen Cottage in Wilberforce. He continued to travel, taking a second trip to Europe in 1881, visiting in England, Scotland, and France, attending meetings, preaching and lecturing and getting re-acquainted with old friends.

As time went on, Daniel faced many new challenges within the AME Church. With so many new churches and new ministers, there were bound to be changes, and Daniel was unhappy with many of them. But now he was not always able to win a majority over to his side. Knowing how hard it had been to raise money for Wilberforce, he thought the AME Church should not open any new college without first having a million dollars on hand. But many new AME colleges started up with very little money, just as Wilberforce had.

Daniel was most upset by the changes he saw in the AME ministry. At the General Conferences in the 1880s, there was a lot of competition among ministers who wanted to be elected bishop and to other high offices in the Church. In Daniel's eyes, General Conferences were becoming too much like political conventions. He also was greatly disturbed because many of the younger ministers did not appear to have the great respect for the office of bishop that he thought they should. He also believed that bishops needed to be holy men and wise, and some of the new bishops did not live up to his expectations.

Nevertheless, Daniel was still held in high regard. At Wilberforce, the Trustees established a theological seminary in 1891. They realized that with the AME Church growing so rapidly, they needed to start training new ministers. They named the new school Payne Theological Seminary and appointed Daniel the first dean. It was especially fitting to name a seminary after the man who had led the AME Church to require that its ministers be formally educated. Payne Theological Seminary is now a separate school with its own Board of Trustees.

Bishop Payne and the ministers who assisted in the organization of the First District Missionary Society, Columbus, Ohio, 1893.

At the General Conference of 1892, the Church set aside one afternoon to celebrate the fortieth anniversary of Daniel's becoming a bishop. Daniel gave his last speech to an AME General Conference, offering advice to the Church and to young ministers. "Do not seek office; if you possess qualification the office will seek you. Do not desire honors; if you are worthy the honors will seek you. Do not desire titles, they have no power to make you wiser, better or more useful."

Daniel spent his last days at his beloved home in Wilberforce. He died on November 29, 1893, at the age of 82. Daniel had been a bishop for forty-one years, longer than any other person in the AME Church, before or since. He had wanted a simple funeral, but there were two elaborate ceremonies, one in Wilberforce, and one at Bethel Church in Baltimore. Three thousand people came to the Baltimore service. At that service, Frederick Douglass, the famous abolitionist, said about Daniel, "His body was small, but his character was large; his voice was feeble, but his words were mighty and powerful; his attainments were great, but his life was greater."

Daniel's friend Francis Grimke, a religious scholar, wrote that Daniel had wanted "to do good, to be useful, to leave the world better than he found it, to be of service to his fellow man." In his remarkable life Daniel had done exactly that. He had been a carpenter, a teacher, a scholar, an abolitionist, a poet, an author of three books and numerous essays, a historian, a pastor, a bishop, and a university president.

During his fifty-two years in the African Methodist Episcopal Church, the little bishop left giant footprints. He played a leading role in shaping Church rules, policies, and forms of worship and he had a powerful influence on the Church's growth and development. Through his exceptional leadership Daniel helped to elevate the AME Church into one of the largest and most influential Black institutions in the world. Today the AME Church has over two million members, eight thousand ministers, and seven thousand congregations around the world.

Daniel was called an "Apostle of Education" because he devoted his life to promoting education for AME ministers, church members, and all African Americans. Fittingly, the seminary named in his honor continues to educate men and women for the ministry. Today the school he fathered, Wilberforce University, enrolls about 850 students. As a member of the United Negro College Fund, it continues to serve mainly African Americans, although students of all faiths and races are welcome. Daniel, who loved "learning more than silver, and wisdom more than gold," would be pleased with the many programs and opportunities Wilberforce offers today. It is a fitting legacy for Daniel Alexander Payne, the man who wished only for "a useful life by Holy wisdom crowned."

DANIEL A. PAYNE'S LEGACY

SCENES FROM TODAY'S WILBERFORCE UNIVERSITY AND PAYNE THEOLOGICAL SEMINARY, THE ENDURING LEGACY OF THE BISHOP WHO FOUGHT SO HARD FOR EDUCATION—FOR AME MINISTERS, FOR CHURCH MEMBERS, AND ALL AFRICAN AMERICANS.

IMPORTANT EVENTS IN THE LIFE OF DANIEL ALEXANDER PAYNE

February 24, 1811	Daniel Alexander Payne born in Charleston, South Carolina
1829	Opens first school
1832	Damages eyesight by observing solar eclipse with naked eye
1834	South Carolina passes law outlawing Daniel's school
May 9, 1835	Sets sail for New York
1835-1837	Studies at Gettysburg Lutheran Theological Seminary
1837	Licensed to preach
1839	Ordained a minister by the Lutheran Church
1837	First Pastorate: "Colored" Presbyterian Church, East Troy, New York
1840	Opens school in Philadelphia
1841	Joins AME Church, unites with Mother Bethel Church
1842	Introduces first resolution calling for educated ministers at Philadelphia Annual Conference
1843-1845	Pastor at Israel AME Church in Washington D.C.
1844	AME General Conference, Pittsburgh. Daniel's resolution requiring AME ministers to be educated written into the Church laws. Daniel leads in establishing Parent and Home Missionary Society
1845-1850	Pastor at Bethel AME Church in Baltimore. Opens last pre-college school. Oversees construction of magnificent new church building. Introduces instrumental music in AME Church
1846	First attempt to go to Europe; ends with terrible storm

1847	Marries Julia Farris. She dies within the year after giving birth
1848	Baby daughter Julia dies
1848	Elected AME Church historian
1852	Elected sixth bishop of the AME Church
1854	Marries Eliza Clark of Cincinnati
1856	Supervises creation of Episcopal Seal with AME Church Motto
1858	Launches and edits magazine *Repository of Religion, Literature, Science and Art*, published until 1862
April 14, 1862	Meets with Abraham Lincoln at the White House
March 10, 1863	Buys Wilberforce University for the AME Church
June 1863	Becomes president of Wilberforce; first Black president of an African-American university
July 3, 1863	Wilberforce opens as AME University; First university owned and operated by African Americans
April 14, 1865	Wilberforce main building burns down
May 1867-May 1868	Daniel travels in Europe
1876	Daniel resigns as president of Wilberforce
1881	Second trip to Europe
1888	Publishes *Recollections of Seventy Years,* his autobiography
1889	Publishes *A Treatise on Domestic Education*
1891	Publishes *History of the African Methodist Episcopal Church*
1891	Payne Theological Seminary established at Wilberforce. Daniel is first dean
November 29, 1893	Daniel Alexander Payne dies. Buried in Laurel Cemetery, Baltimore

AUTHOR'S NOTES AND RESOURCES

The main source of information about Daniel Alexander Payne is his memoir. Unless otherwise noted, quotes in this book come from this source, which is available both through the library and on the Internet:

Payne, Daniel Alexander. 1888. *Recollections of Seventy Years*. Nashville: Publishing House of the AME Sunday School Union. http://docsouth.unc.edu/church/payne70/payne.html

Further background information was gathered from Payne's other writings:

Payne, Daniel Alexander. 1891/1969. *History of the African Methodist Episcopal Church*. Nashville, TN: Publishing House of the AME. Sunday School Union. Reprint ed. New York: Arno Press and the New York Times.

Payne, Daniel Alexander. 1885/1971. *A Treatise on Domestic Education*. Cincinnati: Printed by Cranston & Stowe for the author. Reprint ed. Manchester, NH: Ayer Co.

Payne, Daniel Alexander. 1850. *The Pleasures and Other Miscellaneous Poems*. Baltimore: Sherwood and Co.

One source included entries from the journal Daniel A. Payne kept during his Gettysburg years. Payne's advice quoted on page 61 comes from this source.

Coan, Josephus Roosevelt. 1935. *Daniel Alexander Payne: Christian Educator*. Philadelphia: The A.M.E. Book Concern.

Another useful resource was a book by Hallie Quinn Brown, a student at Wilberforce during the Payne years. She wrote about her first-hand experiences:

Brown, Hallie Quinn. *Pen Pictures of Pioneers of Wilberforce*. Xenia: Aldine, 1937.

Two doctoral dissertations provided helpful perspectives on Payne's life and his significance as an AME bishop and educational leader:

Stokes, Arthur P. 1973. *Daniel Alexander Payne: Churchman and Educator*. Doctoral Dissertation. The Ohio State University.

Tyler, Mark Kelly. 2006. *Bishop Daniel Alexander Payne of the African Methodist Episcopal Church: The Life of a 19th Century Educational Leader*. Doctoral Dissertation. University of Dayton.

Several important documents and images were gathered from the following Internet sources:

The Wilberforce University web site, especially the library archives:

http://www.wilberforce.edu/student_life/library_archives_timeline.html

Documenting the American South, a digital collection of primary source material, sponsored by the University of North Carolina at Chapel Hill.

http://docsouth.unc.edu/

The Library of Congress, American Memory Collections on African American History

http://memory.loc.gov/ammem/index.html

The Digital Collections of the Schomburg Center for Research in Black Culture. The Digital Schomburg:

http://www.nypl.org/research/sc/digital.html

PHOTO CREDITS

Grateful acknowledgments are given to the following sources for supppling photographic images and for permission to reproduce them in this book. Some of the archival items are reproduced from printed materials as the originals were not available. Some items are in the public domain. Genuine attempts have been made to trace the copyright holders of the images and any errors or omissions in credit lines will be made in future printings:

African Methodist Episcopal Church Hymnal, 33t; ©Ricardo Bessin, 13; ©James J. Bishop, 38l, 63c, 63cr, 63br; back cover; Tonya Bolden, 27; ©The Charleston Museum, Charleston, SC, 7b; Chicora Foundation, 7t; © Dickinson College, Special Collections, 23; Fort Sumter National Monument, 49r; ©Gettysburg College, Courtesy of Special Collections/Musselman Library, Gettysburg College, Gettysburg, PA, 22; "History of Bethel AME Church, Pottsville, PA," compiled by Charles A. Williams and Emily Williams Gary, Bethel AME Church, Pottsville, PA, 42; Cheryl Willis Hudson, 4, 21t, 32tr, 55; ©The University of North Carolina at Chapel Hill Libraries, used with Permission of Documenting the American South, 3, 10, 24, 26tl, 31, 32br, 37, 47t; ©Library Company of Philadelphia, 32c; Library of Congress, 1, 2, 9, 16t, 16b, 21b, 25t, 25b, 32tl, 40, 45b, 45r, 49l, 50, 53; ©Missouri Historical Society, 45t; ©Newberry College, courtesy johnbachman.org, 12; ©Ohio Historical Society, iii, 21c, 29, front cover; Ring shout photo by Rutherford, from *Slave Songs of the Georgia Sea Islands, 1942*, by Lydia Parrish, reprinted 1965 by Folklore Associates, Inc., 33b; Wikipedia Foundation, 5; ©Wilberforce University Archives and Special Collections, 17, 19, 47b, 57, 58, 63t, 63r, 63cl, 63bl.

Book design by Edie Weinberg.

INDEX

The Cold War

David Taylor

Heinemann Library
Chicago, Illinois

© 2001 Reed Educational & Professional Publishing
Published by Heinemann Library,
an imprint of Reed Educational & Professional Publishing,
Chicago, IL

Customer Service 888-454-2279

Visit our website at www.heinemannlibrary.com

Designed by AMR
Illustrated by Adrian Barclay and Art Construction
Originated by Dot Gradations

12 11 10 09
10 9 8 7

Library of Congress Cataloging-in-Publication Data
Taylor, David.
    The Cold War / David Taylor.
        p. cm. -- (20th century perspectives)
    Includes bibliographical references and index.
    ISBN 1-57572-434-0 (lib. bdg.)   ISBN 1-58810-373-0 (pbk. bdg.)
1. Cold war--Juvenile literature. 2. World politics--1945-1989--Juvenile literature. [1. Cold war.
2. World politics--1945-1989.] I. Title. II. Series.

D843 .T34 2001
909.82'5--dc21

                                                                                    00-
063458

Acknowledgments
The publisher is grateful to the following for permission to reproduce copyright material:
Bettman/Corbis, p. 16; Corbis, pp. 13, 15, 17, 21, 23, 24, 26, 28, 29, 32, 33, 34, 37, 39, 40;
Corbis/Bettman, p. 6; Corbis/Nasa/Roger Resmeyer, p. 35; Hulton Getty, pp. 19, 31; Popperfoto,
pp. 9, 20, 41; REX, pp. 36, 38, 42; The Art Archive, p. 7

Cover photograph: AKG/Gardi

Special thanks to Christopher Gibb for his comments in the preparation of this book.

Some words are shown in bold, **like this.** You can find out what they mean by looking in the glossary.

Contents

What Was the Cold War?

The United States (U.S.) and the **Union of Soviet Socialist Republics (USSR)** came out of World War II in 1945 as **superpowers.** They were by far the two strongest countries in the world. Although they had fought together against **Nazi** Germany, they soon fell out after the war and became hostile rivals.

THE TWO SIDES IN THE COLD WAR

	The West	**The East**
SUPERPOWERS:	THE UNITED STATES	THE USSR
THEIR ALLIES:	WESTERN EUROPE	EASTERN EUROPE
	IN 1949 THE WEST FORMED AN ALLIANCE OF COUNTRIES CALLED THE NORTH ATLANTIC TREATY ORGANIZATION (NATO).	IN 1955 THE EAST FORMED AN ALLIANCE CALLED THE WARSAW PACT.

Between 1945 and 1989, the two countries and their **allies** were involved in a bitter conflict known as the "Cold War." Like two friends who had argued, the two sides cold-shouldered each other. Periodically, there were confrontations, but the United States and the USSR never used weapons directly against each other. That would have been far too dangerous, as both countries had huge stocks of hazardous nuclear weapons. So, if they did not use weapons against each other, how was the Cold War fought? The diagram below sums up how the Cold War was carried out.

This shows how the West and East fought each other during the Cold War.

U.S.

USSR

SPYING
CIA (U.S.) | KGB (USSR)

INFORMATION
Both sides used television, radio, films, and the press to get across their own point of view.

PROXY WARS
Example: The Arab-Israeli conflict

U.S. supported Israel in the Arab-Israeli conflict by providing money and weapons.

USSR supported the Arabs.

NUCLEAR ARMS RACE
Cruise missile (U.S.)

SS-18 missile (USSR)

Pravda
Capitalism is evil

We disagree

We believe in democracy

PRESTIGE
Each side tried gain prestige by beating the other at sport, e.g. by winning more medals at the Olympic Games

Munich 1972 Olga Korbut, gymnast (USSR Mark Spitz, swimmer (U.S.)

SPACE RACE
Moon landing (U.S.) | Soyuz (USSR)

STRONG WORDS AND THREATS
Carter (U.S.) | Brezhnev (USSR)

This illustrates the main differences between the democratic, capitalist West and the communist East.

Two different types of government

Both sides had a deep mistrust of each other because they believed in different types of government. The countries of the East were run by **communist** governments, whereas the countries of the West had **democratic, capitalist** governments. Both sides thought that their system was the correct one.

The Western countries hated communism and believed that the USSR was out to spread it throughout the world. They, therefore, did everything they could to stop it from spreading. The USSR always denied that it wanted to spread communism and said that the democratic countries were the ones who wanted to dominate the world.

This mistrust made the East and West highly suspicious of each other. Although no shots were fired directly between the two sides, the Cold War hung like a black cloud over the world for about 44 years. People everywhere lived with the fear that a nuclear war could break out at almost any time. When the Cold War came to a sudden and abrupt end in 1989, there was a huge sense of relief.

How Did the Cold War Start?

In 1917, the **Bolshevik Party** took control of Russia and turned it into a **communist** country. Under communism, the Bolsheviks believed that industry would be modernized and the people would have a better standard of living. During the **Russian Civil War** (1918–21), troops from the United States, Britain, Japan, and France were sent to Russia to try and overthrow the new government. They failed and, in 1923, Russia joined with three neighboring areas under Bolshevik control to form the **Union of Soviet Socialist Republics (USSR)**.

In 1941, during World War II, **Nazi** Germany invaded the USSR. The United States, Britain, and the USSR formed the "Grand Alliance" and fought together against Nazi Germany. Even so, distrust was just beneath the surface. Stalin wanted the United States and Britain to open up a **second front** against the Germans in France. They did not do this until 1944. Stalin believed that they had delayed it on purpose to give the Germans the time to inflict heavy losses on the **Red Army.**

The Yalta Conference

By the beginning of 1945, Germany was on the verge of defeat. Soviet troops had pushed the Germans back through Eastern Europe and were closing in on Berlin. From the west, the Americans and British were invading Germany. In February, Stalin, U.S. President Franklin Roosevelt, and Winston Churchill, the British prime minister, met at Yalta on the Black Sea to discuss what would happen at the end of the war. The "big three" decided the following:

The three leaders of the Grand Alliance at the Yalta Conference. From left to right: Stalin, Roosevelt, and Churchill.

1. Each country in Eastern Europe liberated from the Germans by the Red Army would hold free elections.
2. The **United Nations (UN)** Organization would be formed, to stop future wars.
3. When Germany was beaten, the USSR would enter the war against Japan.
4. Germany was to be divided into four zones: Britain, France, the United States, and the USSR would each occupy a zone. As Berlin, the capital, would be in the Soviet zone, it too would be divided into four sectors, with each country taking control of one sector.

Josef Stalin: a ruthless dictator (1879–1953)

The son of a shoemaker, Stalin joined the Bolshevik Party in 1903, and took part in the **Russian Revolution** in 1917. By 1928, he had become leader of the USSR, and within ten years had turned it into a powerful industrial nation. However, his policies were unpopular with many people. In the 1930s, people who opposed Stalin were arrested and put on trial. An estimated eighteen million people were sent to labor camps, half of whom were executed. Stalin was a ruthless dictator who kept a firm grip on the USSR.

The Potsdam Conference

On July 17, 1945, the wartime **allies** met again at Potsdam, outside Berlin. Two of the leaders had changed since Yalta. Clement Attlee was now British prime minister and President Harry S. Truman replaced Roosevelt, who had died on April 12. The three leaders decided to go ahead with the division of Germany and to put the Nazi leaders on trial for war crimes.

There was an uneasy atmosphere at the conference. Truman did not trust Stalin. He was worried because the Soviets had not held any free elections in Eastern Europe. What was Stalin up to? On the other hand, Stalin was alarmed when Truman told him that the United States had exploded the world's first atomic bomb just a day before the conference opened. Stalin was worried that the United States might also use this weapon against the USSR.

The ruins of Hiroshima after it was hit by an atomic bomb on August 6, 1945.

Events in Japan

The Americans did not need Soviet help to defeat Japan. On August 6 and 9, atomic bombs were dropped by the United States on the Japanese cities of Hiroshima and Nagasaki. On September 2, the Japanese signed the terms of surrender on board the *USS Missouri*. The United States was to occupy Japan. It helped to turn Japan into a democratic, independent country. In the years that followed, the U.S. pumped over two billion dollars into Japan so it could rebuild its economy. Meanwhile, in Europe, the seeds of the Cold War had already been sown.

The Iron Curtain Descends

Below is Europe in 1949. Eastern European countries built large barbed-wire fences along their borders with the West.

The **USSR** had suffered badly in World War II. Over 27 million Soviet citizens died and 32,000 factories lay in ruins. Stalin did not want the USSR ever to be invaded again from the west, as it had been by **Nazi** Germany in 1941. He was determined to have friendly countries bordering the USSR. He ordered the **Red Army** to stay in Eastern Europe and put **communist** governments in power in each country. Soon Poland, Romania, Bulgaria, Hungary, Albania, and Czechoslovakia all had communist governments that were willing to take orders from Stalin. Each country became a Soviet **satellite.** Western leaders had hoped that Stalin would hold free elections in each country.

Key
- The Iron Curtain
- Advance of the Red Army 1944–45
- Communist countries
- Communist but not under control of USSR
- Capitalist democratic countries

NB: Austria was occupied by the U.S., USSR, Britain, and France until 1955 when it became independent.

N W E S

NORWAY
SWEDEN
North Sea
DENMARK
Baltic Sea
Moscow
BRITAIN
NETH.
Berlin
Stettin
BELGIUM
EAST GERMANY
POLAND
UNION OF SOVIET SOCIALIST REPUBLICS (USSR)
LUX.
WEST GERMANY
CZECHOSLOVAKIA
FRANCE
SWITZERLAND
AUSTRIA
HUNGARY
Trieste
ROMANIA
YUGOSLAVIA
Black Sea
ITALY
BULGARIA
ALBANIA
GREECE
TURKEY
Mediterranean Sea

0   250 km
0   125 miles

They felt deceived and thought Stalin was blatantly spreading communism across the world. This was a threat to **democracy** and freedom. The mood of mistrust and suspicion deepened between the two sides. In January 1946, Stalin made a speech in which he said that **capitalism** was a threat to world peace. He could not see anything wrong in ensuring that the countries bordering the USSR were friendly and loyal to Moscow. President Truman was concerned about Stalin's attitude and said: "Unless Russia is faced with an iron fist and strong language, another war is in the making."

In March 1946, Truman invited Winston Churchill, the former British prime minister, to visit the United States. Churchill was worried about events in Eastern Europe, and voiced his concerns in public. He made a powerful speech at Westminster College in Fulton, Missouri, saying that Europe was now separated by an "iron curtain" that divided the democratic countries in the West from the communist East.

Churchill's Iron Curtain speech

We understand that Russia needs to be secure on her Western frontiers from all renewal of German aggression. It is my duty, however, to place before you certain facts about the present position in Europe. From Stettin in the Baltic to Trieste in the Adriatic, an iron curtain has descended across the continent. The Communist Parties, which were very small in those eastern states of Europe, have been raised to pre-eminence and power and are seeking everywhere to obtain **totalitarian** *control. This is certainly not the liberated Europe we fought to build up. Nor is it one which contains the essentials of permanent peace.*

Stalin reacted angrily to the speech, saying Churchill was stirring up trouble and that the USSR was merely defending itself from future invasions.

In 1947, Stalin tightened his control on Eastern Europe by introducing the Cominform (Communist Information Bureau). Its job was to coordinate the activities and policies of Communist Parties across Europe. Stalin made sure that all the party leaders were totally loyal and did as Moscow told them. However, Marshal Tito, president of communist Yugoslavia, refused to be ruled by the USSR.

Truman and Churchill drive through the streets of Fulton, Missouri on March 5, 1946. They are on their way to Westminster College, where Churchill was to make his famous Iron Curtain speech.

He argued with Stalin and this led to Yugoslavia being expelled from the Cominform in 1948.

In March 1949, the Western powers formed the North Atlantic Treaty Organization (NATO) to defend themselves from attack. They said that if one member country of the alliance was attacked, the others would help it to fight back. In 1955, the USSR formed a similar alliance called the Warsaw Pact, which was made up of its Eastern European satellites.

MEMBERS OF NATO IN 1955	MEMBERS OF THE WARSAW PACT IN 1955
UNITED STATES	USSR
BELGIUM	ALBANIA
BRITAIN	BULGARIA
CANADA	CZECHOSLOVAKIA
DENMARK	EAST GERMANY
FRANCE	HUNGARY
GREECE	POLAND
ICELAND	ROMANIA
ITALY	
LUXEMBOURG	
NETHERLANDS	
NORWAY	
PORTUGAL	
SPAIN	
TURKEY	
WEST GERMANY	

The Truman Doctrine, 1947

In February 1947, President Truman was faced with a serious problem. In Greece, **communist guerrillas** were trying to take over the country. Britain had 40,000 troops in Greece helping the government fight the communists. Out of the blue, Ernest Bevin, the British foreign minister, told Truman that Britain could no longer afford to keep troops in Greece. Nearby, Turkey was also under threat. The **USSR** had placed troops on the Turkish border, waiting for the right moment to invade.

Truman's dramatic speech

Truman was worried. He feared that communism would spread across the world unless the United States took a stand. He wanted to prevent communism from spreading. On March 12, Truman made a dramatic speech to **Congress.** He said that the United States had to support free people from being taken over by "armed minorities" or "outside pressures." What he meant was that the United States had to stop communists from taking control of **democratic** countries, a policy that became known as the Truman Doctrine. Truman went on to say that communism was an evil system, in which there was no freedom of speech and living standards were low. Congress listened in silence. One member of Congress said that Truman had "scared the hell" out of them. Congress voted the sum of 400 million dollars to support Greece and Turkey. The money helped the Greek government to defeat the communists and keep the USSR out of Turkey.

President Truman makes his historic speech to Congress on March 12, 1947.

The Truman Doctrine

I believe it must be the policy of the United States to support all free peoples who are resisting attempted subjugation [control] by armed minorities or by outside pressures.

President Truman
March 12, 1947

Enter George C. Marshall

In January 1947, General George C. Marshall became the U.S. **secretary of state.** Marshall visited Western Europe in April 1947 and was shocked at the amount of damage caused by World War II. Towns, factories, farms, roads, and railways were still in urgent need of rebuilding, but there was no money to do it. Food was **rationed** and people were living miserable lives. Many countries in Western Europe had communist parties, and the Americans were concerned that people would vote them into power, believing that this would improve their lives.

In June 1947, Marshall made a speech at Harvard University in Massachusetts, in which he said that the United States would give money and equipment to help countries rebuild. This recovery program became known as the Marshall Plan. The offer was open to the USSR and the communist countries of Eastern Europe, but a suspicious Stalin ordered them not to take U.S. money. He said the real aim of the Marshall Plan was to make countries buy U.S. goods, thereby making it even more powerful.

Countries in Western Europe were enthusiastic about the Marshall Plan. Ernest Bevin said it was "like a lifeline to sinking men." By 1952, sixteen countries had received seventeen billion dollars to help them recover from the war. But both the Truman Doctrine and the Marshall Plan had driven a deeper wedge between the West and the East. The Cold War was now a fact of life.

A U.S. cartoon from the time shows the Marshall Plan providing Europe with a lifeline to recovery.

George Catlett Marshall (1880–1959)

Marshall served in the U.S. army in Europe during World War I. From 1939 to 1945 he was chief of staff of the U.S. army. He gained a reputation for being a good organizer.

When he became secretary of state in 1947, President Truman asked him if he could call him George. But Marshall was a believer in formality and he told the startled Truman: "No, General Marshall will do"! Marshall served as U.S. secretary of defense from 1950 to 1951 and was awarded the Nobel Peace prize in 1953.

The Berlin Airlift

At the end of World War II the United States, the **USSR,** Britain, and France divided Germany into four zones. Each country took control of one zone. Berlin, the capital city, was in the Soviet zone. It, too, was divided into four sectors, each under the control of one country. The four countries aimed to work together and, in time, sign a peace treaty with Germany. After this, all occupying troops would be pulled out. But things did not turn out as expected.

Germany had been completely ravaged by the war. Cities and factories lay in ruins. There was a great deal of poverty and food was scarce. The United States and Britain wanted to help their zones recover. Stalin, however, wanted compensation for the damage done to the USSR during the war. He tried to ensure that Germany would never again be strong enough to invade the USSR. The Soviets took factory machinery apart and transported it back to the USSR. They also set up a **communist** government in the Soviet zone.

The Berlin blockade and airlift from 1948 to 1949.

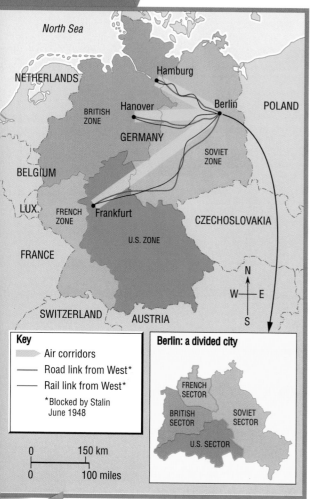

The United States, Britain, and France combined their zones of Germany and sectors of Berlin. Life here began to improve. There was food to buy and goods in the stores. In the Soviet zone, life remained hard. In June 1948, a new kind of money called the Deutschmark was introduced into the Western zones and Berlin. This would help to bring back prosperity to the German people. Stalin did not want anything to do with the new money. He was worried that people in East Berlin would want the same standard of living as people in the West. He decided to try to force the Western powers out of Berlin, so that all of it would be under Soviet control.

Berlin blockaded

Stalin's plan was to try to starve the people of West Berlin. On June 24, 1948, the Soviets closed all roads and railways running from the western half of Germany into Berlin. West Berlin relied on these routes for food and essential supplies, and Stalin hoped that the Western powers would do nothing and leave him in control of Berlin. He was to be disappointed. General Lucius Clay, the U.S. commander in Berlin, said: "If Berlin falls, Western Germany will be next. If we mean to hold Germany against communism, we must not budge."

It was decided to airlift supplies into West Berlin. From June 28, 1948 to May 11, 1949, **USAF, RAF,** and civilian planes made over 275,000 flights in and out of West Berlin, delivering over two million tons of supplies, including food, medicine, coal, clothing, and building supplies. It was a huge undertaking that cost the lives of 79 men. Eventually, Stalin realized that the Western powers were determined to keep West Berlin and he lifted the blockade. Supplies were once again allowed in over land.

The Western **Allies** realized that it was no longer possible to work with the USSR over the running of Germany. They took drastic action. On May 23, 1949, they merged the three Western zones to create the Federal Republic of Germany (West Germany), a **capitalist** and **democratic** country. In October 1949, the USSR reacted by making their Eastern zone the German Democratic Republic (East Germany), a communist country under the influence of Moscow. Germany was to remain a divided country for the next 41 years.

Young children enthusiastically greet the arrival of a U.S. transport plane in Berlin in 1948.

The candy bomber

Lieutenant Gail Halvorsen was a U.S. pilot who took part in the Berlin airlift. He felt sorry for the children of Berlin and wanted to cheer them up. He started "Operation Little Vittles" ("vittles" means food). Halvorsen obtained as many packets of candy and chewing gum as he could, and tied them to small "parachutes" made of handkerchiefs. He and his crew then air-dropped the candy over Berlin. News of the operation spread and soon U.S. candy manufacturers were sending candy to Europe for Halvorsen to drop. By January 1949, he had dropped over 250,000 "parachutes" of candy for the delighted children, who were not used to such treats in postwar Berlin.

Superpower Rivalry, 1945–1969

The arms race

When the United States dropped the first atomic bomb on the Japanese city of Hiroshima on August 6, 1945, it heralded the start of what became known as the arms race. Hiroshima was flattened and 80,000 people were killed instantly. Thousands more died later from **radiation sickness** and burns. The world was shocked by the power of the bomb.

After 1945, as the Cold War started, relations between the West and East worsened. The **USSR** felt insecure, as it did not have the atomic bomb, so Stalin ordered his scientists to produce one quickly. By 1949 they had succeeded. Now it was the turn of the United States and its **allies** to worry; an arms race was under way.

On November 1, 1952, the U.S. exploded the first hydrogen bomb on the Pacific island of Eniwetok. It was a hundred times more powerful than the atomic bomb. On August 14, 1953, the Soviets announced that they, too, had successfully tested a hydrogen bomb. The U.S. president, Dwight Eisenhower, decided that the United States needed to build up a massive stockpile of nuclear weapons. This made economic sense, as they were actually cheaper than **conventional weapons.** One U.S. politician said that nuclear weapons gave "more bang for the buck"!

In 1957, the USSR built the first Intercontinental Ballistic Missile (ICBM). These rockets were able to carry nuclear warheads and could be launched at targets thousands of miles (kilometers) away. The United States soon caught up and by 1958 had its own ICBMs. Missile sites were built in NATO countries close to the USSR, such as Turkey, and pointed at Soviet cities. When the USSR tried to place missiles in Cuba in 1962, it brought the world to the brink of a **nuclear war.** Both sides now had enough weapons to destroy the earth several times over. They had spent vast sums on nuclear weapons that they hoped they would never use. The idea was to deter the other side. If one side attacked, the other would retaliate and the result would be mutually assured destruction (or MAD for short).

The course of an ICBM missile. It would take about 30 minutes for a missile to reach the United States from the USSR. Short-range U.S. missiles based in Turkey would hit the USSR in a matter of minutes.

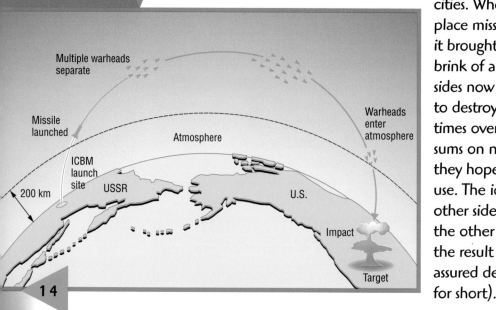

Multiple warheads separate

Missile launched

ICBM launch site   USSR

200 km

Atmosphere

Warheads enter atmosphere

U.S.

Impact

Target

The space race

In 1957 the Soviets launched the world's first satellite into space, and in April 1961 Yuri Gagarin became the first human into space. In a flight lasting 108 minutes, he orbited the earth in a *Vostok* spaceship and returned safely. It was an amazing **propaganda** success for the Soviets, for they claimed that their scientists were in front of those in the West. On February 20, 1962, John H. Glenn became the first American to orbit the earth. In 1963, the Soviets had another success when Valentina Tereshkova became the first woman in space. Which side would be the first to land men on the moon? The Americans won the race when Neil Armstrong and Edwin "Buzz" Aldrin walked on the moon on July 21, 1969.

Edwin "Buzz" Aldrin walks on the moon with the lunar module in the background. Neil Armstrong can be seen reflected in Aldrin's visor.

Nuclear paranoia and protest

During the Cold War, people lived in fear of a nuclear war. Americans built nuclear fallout shelters in their gardens. U.S. schoolchildren were taught fallout drills called "duck and cover." It was said that one hundred Soviet missiles hitting a small island such as Britain would kill 40 million people. In the late 1950s large protest movements evolved, such as the Campaign for Nuclear Disarmament (CND) in Britain, whose members included many eminent scientists, writers, and politicians. Every Easter, CND held a large march from the Atomic Weapons Research Establishment at Aldermaston to London. They called for the government to "ban the bomb." One marcher said: "We're marching because it is all we can do to express our hostility towards a policy that is bound to lead to nuclear catastrophe and widespread destruction." The British government, however, took little notice.

Cold War Spy Scandals

During the Cold War, the level of mistrust was so high that both sides spied on each other to try to gather military secrets and other information. In 1947, President Truman set up the Central **Intelligence** Agency (CIA) whose job was to "collect and coordinate foreign intelligence." Shortly after the death of Stalin in 1953, the **USSR** set up the **KGB** (Committee for State Security) to spy on the West.

Both the CIA and the KGB recruited spies. At the height of the Cold War, each side had up to 4,000 secret agents working for them. One of the earliest spies was Klaus Fuchs, a German-born British scientist. Fuchs was a member of the team that developed the atomic bomb for the United States. In 1950, he was arrested in London for spying for the USSR. He had passed detailed drawings of the bomb to the USSR. This helped the Soviets to build their own atomic bomb much more quickly. Fuchs was imprisoned for fourteen years, but was released in 1959.

A spy in the sky: the U-2 incident, 1960

In early 1960 there was a thaw in the Cold War, when relationships between the two sides began to improve. A summit meeting in Paris was planned for May 14, when it was hoped there would be friendly talks.

On May 1 a U.S. U-2 spy plane, piloted by Francis Gary Powers, was shot down over the USSR. The Soviets found cameras on board the plane and said that Powers had been on a spying mission. They developed the film and found hundreds of photographs of Soviet military bases. President Eisenhower of the United States said that the plane must have gone off course and the cameras had been observing cloud patterns. Khrushchev, the Soviet leader, was furious.

The wreck of the U-2 spy plane piloted by Francis Gary Powers.

When the two leaders met in Paris, Khrushchev demanded a public apology from the United States. Eisenhower refused and the Soviet leader stormed out of the meeting. A planned visit to Moscow by Eisenhower was called off. The thaw was over.

Gary Powers was put on trial in the USSR and sentenced to ten years in prison. He served seventeen months of his sentence before being exchanged with a Soviet spy who was in prison in the United States.

Oleg Penkovsky, a Soviet colonel, spied for the West during 1962–63, providing the United States with details of the USSR's plans during the Cuban Missile Crisis. In 1963, the KGB arrested Penkovsky in Moscow after he was seen with Greville Wynne, his British contact. The USSR claimed that Penkovsky had passed over 500 top-secret military documents to the West. He was executed by firing squad. Wynne was sentenced to eight years in prison.

In 1963, Britain was rocked by the "Profumo Affair." John Profumo was the War Minister in Harold Macmillan's Conservative government. An acquaintance of Profumo was friends with a man named Eugene Ivanov, a diplomat at the Soviet Embassy in London. The British government feared that Profumo had given his acquaintance secret information, which she then passed on to Ivanov. Profumo denied this, but he was forced to resign.

Melita Norwood as seen in September 1999. She said she "gave bomb secrets to the USSR so it could stand up to the West."

Recent scandals

In 1994, Aldrich Ames, a CIA officer, admitted that he had spied for the KGB during the Cold War. He told a court in Virginia, that he had been paid a total of 2.7 million dollars by the KGB for handing over secret information. More seriously, he told the Soviets the names of 25 agents working for the CIA in Moscow. Ten of them were rooted out and shot by the KGB. Ames was sentenced to life imprisonment.

In September 1999, the British public was shocked by the news that an 87-year-old grandmother, Melita Norwood, had spied for the USSR during the Cold War. When she had worked as the personal secretary to the director of the British Non-Ferrous Metals Research Association, Norwood had access to secret documents about Britain's atomic bomb. Code-named "Hola," she passed this information on to the KGB. The British government, however, decided not to prosecute her.

The Korean War, 1950–1953

The main phases of fighting in the Korean War from 1950 to 1953.

Between 1910 and 1945, Korea was controlled by Japan. In 1945, Soviet troops entered Korea north of the 38th parallel of latitude and U.S. troops went into the south. The Japanese were forced to surrender. Like Germany, Korea became a divided country. The Soviets set up a **communist** government in North Korea under the leadership of Kim Il Sung, and in South Korea, an anti-communist government was established under Dr. Syngman Rhee. Both men claimed to be the rightful leader of the whole of Korea. In 1948, Soviet and U.S. troops left and the problem of who should rule Korea was handed over to the **United Nations (UN)**.

War!

On June 25, 1950, North Korean troops invaded South Korea. The Americans were worried that South Korea would be taken over by the North. The United Nations decided to send a force to help the South Koreans. At the time, the Soviets were absent from the United Nations. If they had been there they would have voted against the decision and the UN would not have been able to do anything.

The North Korean army was well-organized and equipped with Soviet-made weapons. It virtually overran South Korea and was closing in on Pusan. On September 15, 1950, UN forces commanded by U.S. General Douglas MacArthur and made up of soldiers from sixteen countries, including the United States, Australia, and Britain, landed at Inchon. By the end of September, the North Koreans had been pushed back over the 38th parallel. MacArthur then drove them northward toward the Yalu River and the Chinese border. China was a communist country and it did not want a U.S.-led UN force so close to its border. So, on October 16, 250,000 Chinese troops were sent to help the North Koreans. The UN forces were pushed back to just south of the 38th parallel.

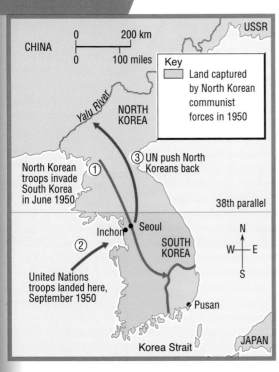

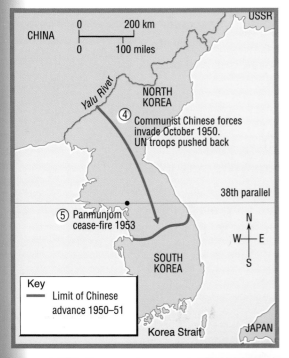

MacArthur dismissed

Truman now wanted an end to the war. The UN forces had expelled the North Koreans from the South and saved it from communism. Truman was satisfied with this. MacArthur, however, wanted to go on with the war. He wanted air strikes against targets in China and said he would consider using the nuclear bomb. Truman knew this was an outrageous idea, as bombing China could bring the **USSR** into the conflict and start World War III. MacArthur still disagreed, so Truman dismissed him. In his farewell speech to **Congress** on April 19, 1951, MacArthur said: "You cannot appease or otherwise surrender to communism in Asia without undermining our efforts to halt its advance in Europe." His words reflected the extreme feelings about communism at the time. Limited fighting went on in Korea for another two years, until in 1953 a cease-fire was agreed at Panmunjom and the war came to end.

U.S. marines launch an artillery attack on the enemy in Korea in 1951.

The results of the Korean War

Korea was still a divided country, but communism had been stopped from spreading into South Korea. The war brought heavy casualties with the United States losing over 50,000 men. Losses of other UN soldiers totaled about 3,200. An estimated one million civilians lost their lives. There was also widespread damage to roads, railways, factories, and towns. Relations between the United States and the USSR were now very strained.

Women in the Korean War

Over 120,000 U.S. women were on service in Korea. Most of them were in the Army Nurse Corps working in Mobile Army Surgical Hospitals. Some served as flight nurses: they flew into war zones to evacuate the injured, tending wounds on the flight back to base. Perhaps the most famous flight nurse was Lillian Kinkela Keil. She flew on over 200 evacuation missions in World War II and came out of retirement to fly on missions in Korea.

Revolution in Hungary, 1956

When Josef Stalin died in 1953, he was replaced by Nikita Khrushchev as the leader of the **USSR.** Stalin had ruled the USSR's **satellite** countries in Eastern Europe with an iron fist. Everyone had to do as Stalin told them or suffer the consequences. Khrushchev, however, seemed to have a more relaxed approach, and talked of existing peacefully side by side with the West.

In February 1956, Khrushchev made a speech in which he said that Stalin had been a brutal tyrant who had used fear and terror to stay in power. People in the countries of Eastern Europe were encouraged by this speech. They thought that Khrushchev would give them more freedom in running their countries and there would be less interference from the USSR.

Riots in Poland

In June 1956, factory workers in Poland rioted when the government raised food prices. The Polish army could not control the rioters, so the USSR sent in tanks to restore order. Khrushchev flew to Poland for talks. He agreed that the popular Vladislav Gomulka should become the Polish leader. The trouble in Poland faded away. But there were more problems waiting for the USSR.

Fighting in Budapest

Hungary had been a Soviet satellite since 1946. The Soviets put a **communist** government into power that answered to the orders of Moscow. Many Hungarians were angry because there was a shortage of food and they were not allowed to criticize the government. People did not like being controlled by the USSR and wanted Soviet troops to get out of Hungary.

A wrecked statue of Stalin in a Budapest street, 1956. This illustrates the Hungarians' anger at Soviet control of their country.

On October 23, 1956, over 300,000 people took to the streets of Budapest, the capital city. They tore down statues of Stalin and demanded greater freedom. The police opened fire as the crowd chanted, "Go home Russians." To please the Hungarians and restore order, Khrushchev allowed the popular Imre Nagy to become the prime minister.

Nagy began to change Hungary. He said that free elections would be held and Hungary would leave the Warsaw Pact. This was too much for Khrushchev. If he allowed Hungary more freedom, then all the other satellite countries would demand the same. He decided to act.

On November 4, 1956, over 6,000 Soviet tanks invaded Hungary to bring the country "back into line." There was heavy street fighting and an estimated 30,000 Hungarians were killed. Budapest suffered heavy damage, with 8,000 houses being destroyed. About 200,000 people fled the country for good. Nagy was arrested and hanged in Moscow in 1958. Khrushchev's message was clear: the USSR would not put up with any of its satellite countries trying to break free of Soviet control.

A Hungarian family, who have fled their home, arrive in Klingenbach in Austria, November 1956.

Escape from Hungary

In 1956, Veronica Varga was a 4-year-old child growing up in Budapest. Her parents decided to flee Hungary, as they were both wanted for "questioning" by the Soviets. On November 28, they boarded a train to take them on the long journey to the Austrian border. The train was virtually empty. The guard told them the train would be searched by Soviet troops when it reached the border. He said they had a better chance of getting across the border if they continued on foot. The train stopped in the countryside and eight passengers, including Veronica and her parents, got off the train. They were met by a group of local farmers and hidden in a barn. The next evening, guided by the farmers, the group set off for the border. Along the way, other people joined them, so that soon the group numbered 50 people. They had to wade through swamps and find their way through thick forests. After about four hours they reached the border, which was protected by a barbed-wire fence, watch-towers, and armed guards. They cut a hole through the fence and crawled through into Austria. People cried tears of joy and sorrow. They were safe, but might never see their homeland, family, and friends again. Veronica and her parents eventually settled in California.

The Berlin Wall Goes Up

After Stalin lifted the blockade in 1949, Berlin remained a divided city. During the 1950s, West Berlin received large amounts of money under the Marshall Plan. This part of the city was rebuilt and soon began to prosper. There was plenty of food in the stores, and there were cinemas, theaters, cafés, and nightclubs. West Berliners could enjoy life again. Above all, they were able to vote in free elections and speak their minds without fear of arrest.

In 1961, the Berlin Wall was built to isolate West Berlin from Soviet territory. The "Country Wall" separated West Berlin from East Germany.

East Berlin, under **communist** rule, was a harsh place. Many buildings remained abandoned and there was very little to buy in the stores. Most people lived in dull apartment blocks and few owned cars, refrigerators, or washing machines, which were becoming common in Western Europe and the United States. East Berliners did not enjoy freedom of speech and lived in fear of being arrested by the secret police. But, despite these differences, people could still travel wherever they liked in the city. Underground trains and trams ran between the East and West. East Berliners were free to visit friends in the West, and over 50,000 of them traveled to work there each day.

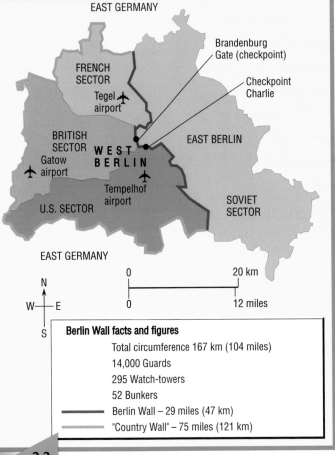

Many East Germans wanted a better standard of living and **defected** to the West. They crossed into West Berlin, where they settled or they caught a plane to West Germany. Most of the defectors were under the age of 45 and many had useful skills. Defectors included teachers, lawyers, doctors, and engineers. There were more job opportunities in the West and wages were higher.

The difference between East and West Berlin showed in clothes. When we went across we always had bags full of things. Like every other family from the West we took fresh fruit which was unobtainable in the East, nicer clothes, and soap. You were always loaded when you went across. In those days there was no Wall, so you didn't have your bags checked. You could cross anywhere where the street went across the border.

Margit Hosseini, a resident of West Berlin, describes life before the Wall went up.

Kennedy and Khrushchev

Soon, more than 200,000 people a year were defecting to the West, and East Germany was losing most of its skilled workers. In June 1961, Nikita Khrushchev, the Soviet leader, met the new president of the United States, John F. Kennedy, in Vienna. Khrushchev thought Kennedy was inexperienced and would crack under pressure. He told Kennedy that he wanted the Western powers out of Berlin by the end of the year or there would be war. Kennedy took him at his word and told the U.S. army to prepare. He also advised Americans to build nuclear shelters.

The Wall

Two months later Khrushchev backed down. He realized that Kennedy was determined to hang on to West Berlin, but somehow he had to put a stop to the flood of people defecting.

Khrushchev and the East German leader, Walter Ulbricht, decided to build a wall that would seal East Berlin off from the West. In the early hours of August 13, 1961, East German workmen started to erect a barbed-wire fence between East and West Berlin. As word spread, people went into the streets to jeer at the workmen, who were protected by armed guards. Near the Brandenburg Gate, in the center of Berlin, a crowd pulled down the barbed wire. Guards turned on water hoses and fired tear gas at the crowd. The East Germans stopped underground trains and trams going into the West. East German workers going to work in the West were turned back by border guards. For a time there was chaos. The Western powers did nothing to stop the Wall being built. Kennedy said, "a wall is better than a war."

Behind the Berlin Wall is the famous Brandenburg Gate, which was built in 1791 as a tollgate for the collection of taxes from people entering the city. The board says: "Attention, you are now leaving West Berlin."

Kennedy visits Berlin

On June 26, 1963, John F. Kennedy visited Berlin. Over one million West Berliners turned out to hear him speak. He gave an inspired speech in which he said the now famous words: "Ich bin ein Berliner." He had meant to say "I am a Berliner," but this actually translates as "I am a doughnut.". . . Nevertheless, the crowd cheered and clapped their approval.

Escaping to the West

When the Berlin Wall was built, it divided friends and families. Before the Wall, people who lived in the West had been able to visit their relations and friends in the East. Now they were permanently separated. Until 1963, they were not even allowed to exchange letters.

Early escapes

In the first days of the Wall there were numerous escapes from the East to West. A Volkswagen car was driven at high speed through the barbed wire, and some people escaped by swimming across the Teltow Canal. In one street, Bernauerstrasse, blocks of apartments backed on to the Wall and some of the residents jumped out of high windows into blankets held by waiting West Berliners. It was not long before East German guards bricked up the windows. Later the apartments were torn down. On August 24, 1961, Gunter Litfin became the first person to be shot dead while trying to escape. Another 40 people were to suffer the same fate over the next twelve months.

East German border guards carry the dead body of Peter Fechter away.

Murderers! Murderers!

On August 17, 1962, seventeen-year-old Peter Fechter and his friend, Helmut Kulbeik, tried to escape over the Wall to the West near the crossing-point, Checkpoint Charlie. The Wall here was built out of cinder blocks and capped with rolls of barbed wire. It was about six and a half feet (two meters) high. They hid in an abandoned house before picking their moment, when they sprinted to the Wall and began to climb it. Unfortunately, they were spotted by the guards, who opened fire with their machine guns. Helmut managed to scramble over the top to safety, but Peter was hit in the back. He slumped to the ground, bleeding heavily. People in West Berlin heard the shooting and stood on car roofs to look over the Wall. They were furious at what they saw and chanted, "Murderers! Murderers!" at the East Germans. Apart from throwing some bandages to him, not one guard tried to help Peter. He lay motionless, screaming for help and in obvious pain. Within an hour, he had bled to death. His body was thrown into a van, which was then driven away by the guards. The whole event was recorded by cameras and shown on television in the West. People were shocked at the brutality of the killing. In West Berlin, there were protest marches and calls for the Americans to bulldoze the Wall down. The calls were ignored and the Wall stayed in place for another 27 years.

Strengthening the Wall

During the 1960s, the East Germans reinforced the Wall, which made it more difficult to escape. The cinder blocks were replaced by solid concrete, for example. Behind the Wall on the Eastern side there was a piece of open ground about 328 feet (100 m) wide, which was known as "death strip." This was overlooked by tall watchtowers and floodlights. Guards with dogs patrolled constantly. It was an awesome barrier. Even so, it did not stop East Germans from trying to escape.

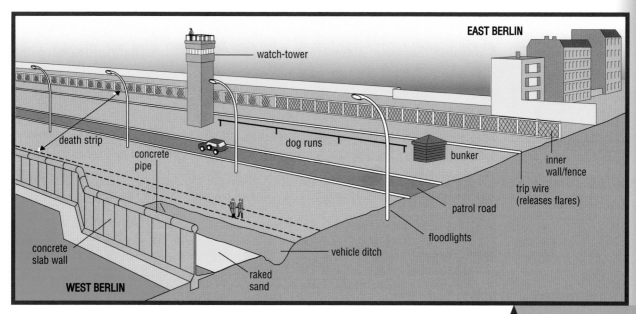

Later attempts at escape

People used many ingenious ways to escape. Some hid in cable drums that were due to be taken to the West. For awhile, people hid in secret compartments in specially built cars, but the guards grew wise to this, so every car entering the West from the East was thoroughly checked. One man hid his girlfriend and mother in his sports car and drove it at high speed under the barrier. The guards were so shocked, they did nothing. Specialist escape organizations were formed: a group led by Wolfgang Fuchs dug seven tunnels under the Wall through which about 500 people were guided to freedom. The longest tunnel was 394 feet (120 m) long and even had lighting and ventilation. Another escape organizer, Wolf Quasner, specialized in forging diplomatic passports and visas. These were smuggled into East Berlin and sold to people who wished to escape to the West.

As the years wore on, fewer attempts were made to escape. Life in East Berlin improved a little as wages rose and people could afford to buy a few home comforts, such as televisions and washing machines.

The Berlin Wall was heavily fortified, making it almost impossible to cross.

The Cuban Missile Crisis, 1962

Since 1898, U.S. firms had controlled most of Cuba's economy. The United States also had a large naval base at Guantánamo in southeast Cuba. In 1959 Fidel Castro overthrew Fulgencio Batista, the corrupt Cuban leader. The new government immediately took control of all industry and businesses, most of which had been owned by Americans. This angered the Americans and in 1961 they supported an invasion of Cuba, the aim of which was to remove Castro from power. About 1,500 exiled Cubans landed at the Bay of Pigs, but were easily beaten by Castro's troops. Castro's dislike of the United States deepened and he made friends with Khrushchev, who was happy to send him money and arms. Castro then announced that Cuba was to be a **communist** country.

Crisis

On October 14, 1962, Major Richard Heyser's U–2 spy plane flew over Cuba and photographed Soviet nuclear missile sites being built. The threat to the United States was obvious, as Cuba is just 93 miles (150 km) away from Florida's coast. From there, Soviet missiles could be fired at most U.S. cities.

Soviet missile sites on Cuba as photographed by a U–2 plane. The photograph was taken from 34 miles (4,500 m) up in the air, but was so accurate that it was possible to read the writing on the side of the missiles!

An alarmed President Kennedy called together a committee of twelve advisers to discuss what action should be taken. Kennedy secretly recorded the conversation, and the tape shows the drama of the occasion. The committee had three stark choices:

1. Bomb the missile bases and other targets in Cuba.
2. Invade Cuba.
3. Put a naval blockade around Cuba to stop Soviet ships from delivering missiles.

The **USAF** told Kennedy that an air strike could cost up to 20,000 lives. After a drawn-out argument it was decided to blockade Cuba. Any ships heading for Cuba with cargoes of "offensive weapons" would be turned back. Some members of the committee thought that Kennedy was being soft. For example, General LeMay told him: "I just don't see any other solution except direct military action right now. A blockade would be considered by a lot of our friends to be a pretty weak response."

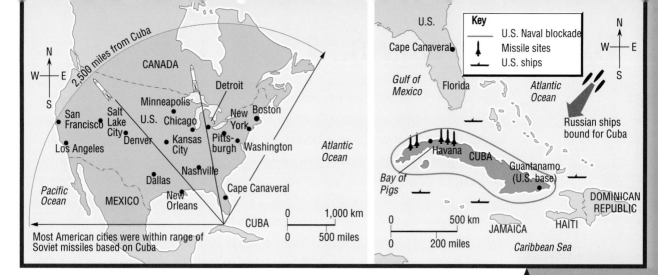

On the left map:

2,500 miles from Cuba

CANADA

Detroit

Minneapolis

San Francisco · Salt Lake City · U.S. · Chicago · New York · Boston

Denver · Kansas City · Pitts-burgh · Washington

Los Angeles

Nashville

Dallas

New Orleans · Cape Canaveral

Pacific Ocean · MEXICO

CUBA

Atlantic Ocean

0 1,000 km
0 500 miles

Most American cities were within range of Soviet missiles based on Cuba.

On the right map:

U.S.

Cape Canaveral

Gulf of Mexico · Florida

Atlantic Ocean

Key
— U.S. Naval blockade
↓ Missile sites
— U.S. ships

Russian ships bound for Cuba

Havana · CUBA

Bay of Pigs

Guantanamo (U.S. base)

DOMINICAN REPUBLIC

JAMAICA · HAITI

Caribbean Sea

0 500 km
0 200 miles

On October 24, U.S. warships blockaded Cuba to wait for the Soviet ships they knew were on their way. Would the Soviets try to break the blockade or would they turn back? The world held its breath. Thankfully they stopped and turned back. But there was still the question of what to do about the missiles already sited on Cuba.

On October 26, Khrushchev, the Soviet leader, wrote to Kennedy saying he was willing to remove the missiles if Kennedy guaranteed that the United States would not invade Cuba. Before Kennedy had a chance to answer, on October 27 a second letter arrived from Khrushchev. This one demanded that the United States remove the missiles it had placed in Turkey. Kennedy was puzzled. How should he reply? His brother Robert, the U.S. **attorney general,** advised him to ignore the second letter and just reply to the first. President Kennedy took the advice and told Khrushchev that he would not invade Cuba. On October 28, Khrushchev announced on Radio Moscow that he would remove the missiles from Cuba. Castro was furious that Khrushchev withdrew the Soviet missiles from Cuba without asking him first, but the crisis was over.

If Khrushchev had not backed down, the world could have been plunged into a **nuclear war,** but many people in the **USSR** thought their country had lost face. People in the West were grateful that Khrushchev had not pushed the United States any further and that a potential World War III had been avoided.

As a result of the crisis, a direct telephone "hot line" was put in between the Kremlin in Moscow and the White House. This would enable the leaders of the United States and USSR to talk directly to each other, rather than having to correspond by letter. In 1963, both sides signed the Test Ban Treaty, which was supposed to stop the testing of nuclear bombs in the atmosphere, underwater, and in space.

The Cuban Missile Crisis, 1962. The Soviet missiles had a range of 2,600 miles (4,183 km). The map shows how far across the United States this would reach and how the United States blockaded Cuba.

Monday October 29, 1962

NEW YORK MIRROR

K BOWS!
Will Pull Out Missiles
Kennedy Made No Deals

How the New York Mirror reported the end of the Cuban Missile Crisis. "K" was the U.S. nickname for Krushchev.

The Prague Spring, 1968

Czechoslovakia had **communism** imposed upon it in 1948. From that moment, no other political parties were allowed and the country came under the influence of the **USSR.** Following the example of the Soviets, Czech industry concentrated on producing steel and coal. Very few household goods such as furniture, cameras, radios, and fashionable clothes were produced, so the Czech people had a low standard of living. Wages were lower than in the West and for many people life was drab. Under the communists, if anyone criticized the government they would be thrown into prison. Newspapers and the movies were **censored** and there were no free elections.

The people of Prague try to persuade Soviet tank crews to go home, August 1968.

In 1967, there was a slump in trade. Factories were forced to cut down on production, and wages were lowered. Antonin Novotny, the hard-line Czech leader, did nothing to improve the situation. In January 1968, Novotny was dismissed by the Communist Party and replaced as leader by Alexander Dubček.

Reforms

Dubček wanted Czechoslovakia to stay a communist country loyal to Moscow, but he believed that people should have more freedom and a higher standard of living. He called it communism "with a human face." In March 1968 Dubček announced a number of reforms. Newspapers would no longer be censored and people would be free to criticize the government if they wished. Dubček also promised that political parties other than the Communist Party would be allowed. Czech people would be able to travel abroad more, and people who had been imprisoned for criticizing the government were released. These reforms became known as the Prague Spring.

Invasion

The Soviet leader, Leonid Brezhnev, was worried by events in Czechoslovakia. Recalling the events in Hungary in 1956, he feared that if the Czech people were given more freedom the other **satellite** countries would want the same. Brezhnev did not trust Dubček and believed Dubček would take Czechoslovakia out of the Warsaw Pact. The time had come for action. On August 21, 1968, over 500,000 Soviet troops supported by smaller units from Poland, Hungary, East Germany, and Bulgaria invaded Czechoslovakia. Crowds of people went into the streets of the capital city, Prague, to confront the Soviet tanks. The famous Czech Olympic athlete, Emil Zatopek, made an emotional speech, saying that the Russians should go home. Some tanks were set on fire but, in general, the protesters stayed calm. Some people climbed onto the tanks to ask the soldiers to go home.

Dubček, however, was arrested and taken to Moscow. He was made to give up his program of reforms and had to agree to Soviet troops staying in Czechoslovakia. In 1969, Gustav Husak, a hard-line communist, replaced Dubček as leader. The Soviets knew that Husak would do as Moscow told him.

By invading Czechoslovakia, Brezhnev made it clear that he was going to keep Eastern Europe firmly under Soviet control. He issued the Brezhnev Doctrine, which said that if one satellite country tried to move towards **democracy,** it was the duty of other communist countries to stop it.

A large crowd turned out to pay their last respects to Jan Palach, January 1969.

Jan Palach

On January 19, 1969, Jan Palach, a 21-year-old Czech student, set fire to himself in Wenceslas Square in Prague. He was protesting against the Soviet invasion and the fact that Dubček's reforms had been abolished. Palak died from his injuries on January 21. A huge crowd of 800,000 turned out to watch his funeral in Prague. They shouted, "Russians go home." It was an emotional occasion and gave people the chance to vent their hatred of the USSR.

Two months later there were great celebrations when the Czech ice-hockey team beat the USSR 4–3 in the World Ice Hockey Championships in Stockholm, Sweden. An audience of six million Czech people watched the match on television. They looked upon the victory as revenge against the Soviet invaders.

War in Vietnam

During the late nineteenth century, French troops conquered Vietnam, in Southeast Asia, and it remained a French colony until the outbreak of World War II. In 1940, the Japanese forced the French out of Vietnam, but they returned in 1946. A **communist** group called the **Vietminh,** led by Ho Chi Minh, drove them out for good in 1954.

At a conference in Geneva, Vietnam was split into two separate countries: North Vietnam with a communist government headed by Ho Chi Minh, and South Vietnam with an anti-communist government. The conference intended free elections to be held in 1956, and that the winner would rule a united Vietnam, but the elections were never held.

The government in South Vietnam soon became very unpopular. It was made up of greedy landowners who did nothing to help the peasant farmers. The government came under attack from **Vietcong guerrilla** soldiers supported by the communist North. The Americans believed that North Vietnam wanted to take over the South and turn the whole of Vietnam into a communist country. They felt that if Vietnam fell to communism, other countries in Southeast Asia would follow, rather like a row of upright dominoes being toppled.

A map of Southeast Asia during the Vietnam War.

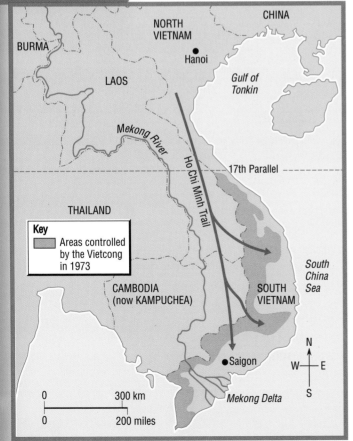

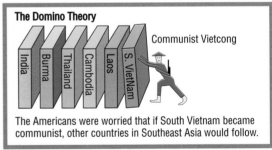

The Domino Theory

Communist Vietcong

India | Burma | Thailand | Cambodia | Laos | S. Vietnam

The Americans were worried that if South Vietnam became communist, other countries in Southeast Asia would follow.

So, the United States sent money and advisers to help the government of South Vietnam fight the Vietcong. Gradually, the Vietcong won the support of many South Vietnamese peasants, and by 1961 they controlled over half of South Vietnam. North Vietnam supplied the Vietcong with weapons which were carried down a jungle track called the Ho Chi Minh Trail. In 1962, President Kennedy sent U.S. troops to help the South Vietnamese. When Kennedy was assassinated in 1963, Lyndon Johnson became president of the United States.

Johnson steps up the war

In 1964, North Vietnamese gunboats fired on a U.S. warship, *USS Maddox* in the Gulf of Tonkin. **Congress** gave Johnson permission to step up the war. In 1965, B-52 bombers began "Operation Rolling Thunder," a series of bombing raids on the North. Over a three-year period more bombs were dropped on Vietnam than by all the sides in World War II. By 1968, there were over 500,000 U.S. troops in Vietnam. The Vietcong, however, were difficult to fight. They hid in the jungle and carried out surprise attacks. They did not wear a uniform so it was impossible to tell them apart from ordinary peasants. On January 30, 1968, the Vietcong launched the Tet Offensive, a major attack on Saigon and other South Vietnamese cities. The attack took the U.S. troops by surprise. Although the Vietcong were eventually driven back, many Americans came to believe that the war should be brought to an end.

In 1969 Richard Nixon, the new U.S. president, promised to scale down the United States' involvement in the war. He began to withdraw troops and provided South Vietnam with weapons to defend itself. Nixon said he would seek "peace with honor." In 1973, the Paris Peace Agreement was signed which ended the United States' participation in Vietnam. By 1975, North Vietnamese troops had overrun the South. Vietnam became a united country under a communist government.

A U.S. B-52 bomber in action during the Vietnam War. These bombers flew at a height of nine miles (15,000 meters) up in the air and carried 28 bombs, each weighing more than two tons.

WAR FACTS

U.S. SOLDIERS KILLED	58,132
AUSTRALIAN SOLDIERS KILLED	501
NORTH VIETNAMESE AND VIETCONG SOLDIERS KILLED	900,000
SOUTH VIETNAMESE SOLDIERS KILLED	200,000
CIVILIANS KILLED	500,000
COST TO U.S. TAXPAYERS	$150 BILLION
COST TO AUSTRALIAN TAXPAYERS	$218.4 MILLION

LARGE AREAS OF VIETNAMESE FOREST AND FARMLAND WERE DESTROYED OR POISONED BY CHEMICALS.

Americans Protest

When the U.S. government first got involved in Vietnam it had the support of the majority of the population. Those who opposed the war were **pacifists** or members of religious groups. In November 1965, Norman Morrison, a strict **Quaker,** set fire to himself near the Pentagon building in Washington, D.C. He died from his burns. Morrison had read a report about innocent Vietnamese villagers being burned by napalm dropped by U.S. planes. He felt so bad about this that he was driven to take his own life in protest. The nation was shocked by Morrison's death. Opposition to the war had started to gain momentum.

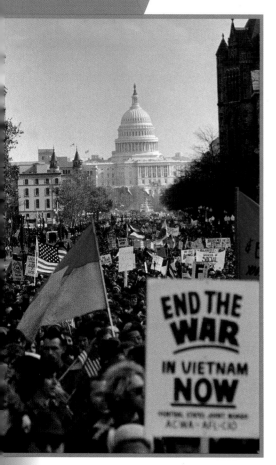

Anti-Vietnam War protesters march down Pennsylvania Avenue toward a rally at the Washington Monument in 1969.

In April 1965, a group called Students for a Democratic Society organized a protest in Washington, D.C. attended by 20,000 people. A "teach-in" was held at the University of Michigan, where people discussed the war and whether the United States should be involved in it. Superstar singers such as Joan Baez and Bob Dylan wrote songs protesting against the war.

The war escalated as the 1960s wore on and more and more Americans were drafted (enlisted) into the army to serve in Vietnam. Most of them were from the working class rather than the middle class. Twenty percent of the draftees were African-American, yet they only made up ten percent of the U.S. population.

The horrors of war brought home

The war was widely reported. Every day people watched the news on television. They began to question why the United States had got itself into such a terrible war. Thousands of young Americans were being killed: in one week in May 1968, 5,550 U.S. soldiers were killed.

The protests in the United States became more defiant and militant. Men drafted to fight refused to go to Vietnam. Many burned their draft papers in public. Others fled the country and went to Canada to avoid being sent to Vietnam. The world heavyweight boxing champion,

Muhammad Ali, refused to serve in the army and was stripped of his world title, but his action inspired others to resist the draft. Demonstrations often turned violent as protesters clashed with the police. In 1969, the U.S. public was shocked to learn about the killing of over 300 civilians by U.S. troops in My Lai, a village in South Vietnam. This fueled opposition to the war. One political commentator said: "How can we Americans support actions like this?"

The protests continued, with students strongly voicing their anti-war feelings. On May 1, 1970, Nixon said that student protesters were "bums" who should get on with their studying. Three days later, tragic events took place at Kent State University.

Tragedy at Kent State University, Ohio

On April 30, 1970, there was anger in the United States when Nixon secretly ordered U.S. troops to invade Cambodia. On May 4, students at Kent State University, near Cleveland, Ohio, held an anti-war demonstration. National Guardsmen fired their guns into the crowd, killing four students. Two of them were on their way to class and were not even part of the demonstration. Anger and fury spread across the United States. There were strikes at almost 500 universities and the rock band, Crosby, Stills, Nash & Young recorded a song called "Ohio." A commission was set up to investigate the killings. In its report it said: "A nation driven to use the weapons of war upon its youth is a nation on the edge of chaos."

A horrified student holds her head in anguish as she looks at one of the dead students lying in a pool of blood.

By now soldiers were deserting the army, while others sewed peace badges onto their uniforms. In the United States, the GIs Against the War Movement was formed. They argued that the war was a fiasco and immoral. They said: "We are forced to fight in a war we did not create and in which we don't believe." In 1973, the Americans withdrew their last troops from Vietnam. The protest movement had played its part in the United States' decision to end the war.

Détente, 1968–1979

Between about 1968 and 1979 there was a period of **détente** between the United States and the **USSR.** During this time, both sides tried to be more friendly toward each other and there was less tension. There were several reasons for this. By 1968, they each had about the same number of nuclear weapons and they knew that a major war would destroy the planet. President Nixon felt it was time to be friendlier toward the USSR to try to reduce the threat of **nuclear war.** The USSR, under Leonid Brezhnev, also wanted friendlier relations. The money spent on nuclear weapons would be better spent on improving living conditions in the USSR.

Then there was the issue of China, the world's biggest **communist** country. In 1960 the USSR and China fell out. This suited the West, as the spread of communism would have been a much bigger threat if the USSR and China were **allies.** Nixon made every effort to be friends with China. The USSR, in turn, wanted to be friendly with the United States so that it had an ally against China. Finally, all three countries knew that they could earn money by increasing trade with each other.

Détente in action

In 1968 the Non-Proliferation Treaty, which aimed to stop the spread of nuclear weapons, was signed by the United States, the USSR, and Britain. They agreed that they would not help other countries to build nuclear weapons. Another 59 countries promised not to make them. Unfortunately France, Israel, South Africa, and China refused to sign the treaty. Between 1969 and 1972 the Strategic Arms Limitation Talks (SALT) were held, which resulted in an agreement that became known as SALT I. The United States and the USSR agreed to limit the number of long-range nuclear missiles they would produce over the next five years.

Nixon and Brezhnev sign the SALT I agreement in Moscow in May 1972. The agreement helped to produce friendlier relations between the United States and the USSR.

The most dramatic example of détente in action was a joint U.S.–Soviet space mission in July 1975. Two spacecraft, the Soviet *Soyuz* and the U.S. *Apollo*, docked 155 miles (250 km) above the earth. The two crews shared meals and carried out experiments together. It was a momentous event, and it appeared to point toward a new era of friendliness between the countries. Another breakthrough came on August 1, with the signing of the Helsinki Agreements. Thirty-five countries, including the United States and the USSR, agreed to recognize the 1945 borders of Eastern Europe. They also agreed that all people should have basic human rights: the right to "freedom of thought, religion and belief."

The U.S. astronaut Deke Slayton and the Soviet cosmonaut Alexei Leonov meet each other in space, July 17, 1975.

Relations begin to break down

However, the old distrust between the West and East was still there, and rivalry between the two sides continued. In the Arab–Israeli war of 1973, the Soviets sent aid to the Arabs and the Americans supported the Israelis. Neither side would let inspectors into their country to check the number of nuclear weapons. This left each side suspicious as to whether the other was actually destroying weapons as it had promised.

The Soviets continued to deny their citizens basic human rights. A group of **dissidents** led by Andrei Sakharov, a famous scientist, protested to the government about prison conditions and called for people to be able to travel freely outside the USSR. Sakharov was placed under house arrest. In Afghanistan, a Muslim group, the **Mujaheddin,** rebelled against the government of President Hafizullah Amin. In December 1979, the USSR sent troops into Afghanistan to "restore order." They put a communist government into power that was loyal to Moscow. The Western powers were furious. The invasion brought détente to an end.

Richard Nixon

Richard Nixon was born in California in 1913. He was a **Republican** and became president of the United States in 1969. Nixon was a strong supporter of détente and said that the United States "extended the hand of friendship to the Soviet and Chinese people." He was the first U.S. president to recognize communist China and its leader, Mao Zedong. In 1972 Nixon visited Beijing and Moscow for talks. He took the United States out of Vietnam in 1973, but was forced to resign over the **Watergate** scandal in 1974, and was replaced by Gerald Ford.

Cold War Again

The U.S. president, Jimmy Carter, was angered and dismayed by the Soviet invasion of Afghanistan. He said it was "the greatest threat to world peace since World War II." Relations cooled between the United States and the **USSR** and attitudes hardened once again. Carter immediately stopped U.S. exports of grain to the USSR and **Congress** cancelled the SALT II agreement that had been signed in 1979. This agreement, based on talks that had been going on since 1972, would have further limited the production of nuclear missiles. Instead, Carter increased the size of the U.S. military and allowed the production of a new missile system to go ahead.

In July 1980, the United States and 60 other nations boycotted the Olympic Games in Moscow in protest at the Soviet occupation of Afghanistan. The Soviets retaliated by telling people that there would be CIA agents in the crowd giving away poisoned chewing gum!

The evil empire

On January 21, 1981, Ronald Reagan replaced Carter as U.S. president. Reagan, a **Republican,** was strongly opposed to **communism.** He called the USSR an "evil empire." He wanted to push back communism and win the Cold War battle. Reagan adopted an aggressive stance towards the USSR and its **allies,** and used strong language in his speeches. In 1983, he said that the Cold War was a "struggle between freedom and **totalitarianism,** between what is right and wrong." Under Reagan, **cruise missiles** were placed in NATO countries in Europe, and the United States stopped trading with the USSR.

Supporters of the Campaign for Nuclear Disarmament (CND) protest against cruise missiles outside Greenham Common air base in England, 1983.

Nuclear protests

In 1982, it was announced that cruise missiles were to be sited in Britain, at Greenham Common in Berkshire. The news was met with widespread opposition in Britain. On December 12, 1982, over 30,000 women formed a human circle around the Greenham Common air base. The women attached a token from their lives onto the perimeter fence. Many chose to pin up photographs of their children. Other tokens included diapers, anti-war poems, and teddy bears. On April 1, 1983, thousands of people protested by joining hands to form a 14-mile (22-kilometer) human chain stretching from the Atomic Weapons Research Establishment at Aldermaston to Greenham Common. Large numbers of women set up a peace camp on the outside of the air base and kept up a daily vigil of protest.

Star Wars

Reagan was frightened that the USSR might launch a nuclear attack on the United States, so in 1983 he introduced the Strategic Defense Initiative (SDI), known as "Star Wars." It was a system that aimed to interrupt foreign missiles, using laser beams fired from satellites in space. It took the arms race almost into the realm of science fiction. Once it was perfected, SDI would provide the United States with the means to survive a first strike attack and enable it to fire missiles back. It would have put the Americans well ahead of the USSR, but was very expensive to develop. Not surprisingly, U.S. defense spending increased from 178 billion dollars in 1981 to 367 billion dollars in 1986. Reagan also sent money to groups fighting left-wing governments in Afghanistan, Nicaragua, El Salvador, and Angola.

Once again there was great tension between East and West. In 1984 the USSR boycotted the Olympic Games, which were held in Los Angeles. It appeared that the two sides would never be friendly again. Few would have imagined the changes that were to occur after 1985.

James Earl (Jimmy) Carter

Carter was born in 1924 in Plains, Georgia. After a career in the U.S. navy, he went back to Georgia and became a peanut farmer. In 1971 Carter, a **Democrat,** was elected governor of Georgia. Six years later, in 1977, he became president of the United States. As president, he persuaded Egypt and Israel to sign a historic peace treaty and was a supporter of human rights. The Afghanistan crisis forced him to take a hard line against the USSR.

President Reagan makes a joke at a press conference to explain the workings of SDI. The SDI helped rekindle the tension between the United States and the USSR.

Enter Mikhail Gorbachev

In 1985 Mikhail Gorbachev became the Soviet leader. He said that the **USSR** had been stagnating since 1982 under the rule of Leonid Brezhnev and that it was time for change. Gorbachev believed in **communism** but thought people should be given more freedom. His ideas were similar to those of Alexander Dubček, who had tried to introduce changes into Czechoslovakia in 1968. Gorbachev announced the twin policies of *perestroika* and *glasnost*. By *perestroika*, Gorbachev meant that he was going to rebuild the Soviet economy so that there would be more goods in the stores at cheaper prices. He said that Soviet factories were expert at building rockets but could not make a decent washing machine. *Glasnost* meant there would be more "openness" and that there would be freedom of speech in the USSR. People would be allowed to discuss politics and criticize the government.

A Soviet SS–20 intermediate range missile being destroyed in 1988.

If the Soviet people were to have a better standard of living, the USSR would need to spend far less on weapons and nuclear missiles. Gorbachev realized that the only way to achieve this was to make friends with the West again and talk about disarmament. He wanted **capitalism** and communism to live peacefully side by side.

On November 21, 1985, Gorbachev met President Ronald Reagan in Geneva. The two men talked for six hours about the Cold War and how the West and East could make a fresh start. Afterward, Gorbachev said that the two men had got on well and the world had become a safer place. People in the West warmed to the Soviet leader. They liked his honesty and cheerful personality. Slowly, trust was replacing mistrust.

In October 1986, the two **superpower** leaders met again in Reykjavik, Iceland. They agreed to scrap some of their nuclear missiles but then Gorbachev said he wanted Reagan to stop the Strategic Defense Initiative ("Star Wars") program. Reagan refused, but invited Gorbachev to visit the United States at a later date. Gorbachev remained positive and invited Western leaders to visit the USSR. In March 1987, the people of Moscow gave Margaret Thatcher, the British prime minister, an enthusiastic welcome.

The breakthrough in arms reduction finally came at a summit meeting in Washington, D.C. in December 1987 when Reagan and Gorbachev signed the Intermediate Nuclear Forces Treaty. Both sides agreed to destroy all missiles that had a range of between 310 and 3,441 miles (500 and 5,550 km). To make sure that they were doing as they promised, teams of inspectors were allowed to count the number of missiles. It looked as though the Cold War was coming to an end.

Reagan visited Moscow in June 1988, where he praised Gorbachev's attitude, saying that their talks had made "huge breaches in the walls of the Cold War fortress." And this was from a man who five years before had called the USSR "an evil empire." In December 1988, Gorbachev told the **United Nations (UN)** that he would cut the Soviet army by ten percent, or 500,000 soldiers.

Gorbachev's efforts to end the Cold War made him very popular in the West. The newspapers called it "Gorby Mania." But in the **satellite** countries of Eastern Europe, people saw a chance to break free from the USSR. The year 1989 was to see dramatic changes in Eastern Europe.

Mikhail and Raisa Gorbachev leaving a polling station after voting in a local election in Moscow, March 18, 1990.

Raisa Gorbachev

Raisa Maximovna Titorenko was the daughter of a railway worker. Born in 1932, she was a brilliant student. She gained a place at Moscow University, where she met Mikhail Gorbachev. They married in 1955. When her husband became the Soviet leader, Raisa gave him all the support she could. He nicknamed her "My General" and said that he always asked for her views before making a decision. Raisa was known for her warmth and confidence, and was always immaculately dressed. The heavy workload of her husband caused her to worry. "His worries are also my worries," she said. In August 1991, Raisa suffered a stroke, followed by a heart attack in 1993. The "first lady of Soviet chic" died of leukemia in Sept 1999, at the age of 67.

1989: Year of Revolutions

The countries of Eastern Europe had been under the control of the **USSR** since 1945. Attempts to break free, for instance in Hungary (1956) and Czechoslovakia (1968), had been crushed by the Soviet army. In March 1989, Mikhail Gorbachev said that the USSR would never again use force to impose its will on the countries of Eastern Europe. He also said that he would begin to withdraw Soviet troops from Eastern Europe, giving people the freedom to choose the kind of government they wanted.

The communist leaders of Eastern European countries were dismayed, but the ordinary people sensed that the time was right to end **communism** and break away from the USSR. People were tired of communism: it had failed to bring them a comfortable standard of living and did not allow basic human rights. They looked with envy at the wealth and freedoms of the **democratic** countries in the West. By the end of 1989, communism had completely collapsed in Eastern Europe. It was an amazing turnaround.

A man smashes down the Berlin Wall in November 1989. The bemused guards can only stand and watch. The Wall had been a hated symbol of the Cold War for 28 years.

In May, the Hungarian government took down the barbed-wire fence that bordered noncommunist Austria. Thousands of East Germans traveled to Hungary, crossed into Austria and went on into West Germany. There was nothing anyone could do to stop them. In Poland, which had been the first Soviet **satellite** to defy Moscow in the early 1980s, the trade union Solidarity beat the communists in elections. The Solidarity leader, Lech Walesa, later became president of a democratic country.

The Berlin Wall comes down

The East German leader, Erich Honecker, wanted to hold on to power, but was very unpopular. On October 7, Gorbachev visited East Berlin and told the people "to take democracy if they wanted it." On October 9, there was a mass march of 100,000 people in the East German city of Leipzig, calling for elections.

The momentum was for change. On October 18, Honecker was forced to resign and was replaced by Egon Krenz, a moderate communist. Krenz said that people were free to travel to the West if they wanted. The East Germans took this to mean that the Berlin Wall had been opened. On the night of November 9, thousands of people flocked to the Wall and they demanded to be let through to West Berlin. As they walked through the checkpoint, the confused border guards could only stand and watch. There were wild scenes of rejoicing. Hundreds climbed onto the Wall and began to hack it to pieces. Berlin was no longer a divided city.

On November 10 the communist leader in Bulgaria resigned. One week later, on November 17, in Prague, Czechoslovakia, police brutally beat up people who were protesting against the communist government. There followed a week of massive demonstrations in which people called for democracy. On November 24, the government resigned. There was hardly any bloodshed, so the overthrow of the communist regime became known as the "Velvet Revolution." Vaclav Havel, a famous playwright who had long opposed communism, became the new president of a democratic Czechoslovakia. Finally, in December communism came to a violent end in Romania.

The body of Nicolae Ceausescu, as shown on Romanian television. The Romanian people were pleased to see his downfall.

Death of a tyrant

Nicolae Ceausescu became the leader of Romania in 1967. He refused to be dominated by Moscow. He visited the United States in 1972 and Britain in 1978. Little did the people of Western Europe realize at the time what a tyrant they were befriending. Anyone who dared to criticize Ceausescu was arrested by the Securitate (secret police), imprisoned, and tortured. On December 17, 1989, there was a demonstration against Ceausescu in the town of Timisoara. People called out, "We want bread" and "Down with Ceausescu." The secret police opened fire and killed thousands of people. On December 22, Ceausescu called a public meeting in Bucharest to show the people that he was in control. The crowd booed him and threw stones. The next day he and his wife fled Bucharest in a helicopter. The Ceausescus were soon caught by the army, put on trial, and on December 25, executed by firing squad.

The End of the Cold War

On a stormy morning on December 2, 1989, U.S. President George H. W. Bush and the Soviet leader Mikhail Gorbachev met on board the *Maxim Gorky*, a Soviet warship, off the coast of Malta. They formally announced that the Cold War was over. Further talks on reducing nuclear weapons were to be held, and trade links between the United States and the **USSR** strengthened. In 1991 the Strategic Arms Reduction Treaty (START) was signed, which reduced the number of Soviet nuclear missiles by 5,000 and U.S. ones by 3,500.

> *I do not regard the end of the Cold War as a victory for one side. The end of the Cold War is our common victory.*
> Mikhail Gorbachev

The breakup of the USSR

By 1990, Gorbachev had become very unpopular in the USSR. *Perestroika* was not working. Prices were high and ordinary goods were in short supply. People still had to stand in line for hours to buy food. Some politicians inside the **Communist** Party did not like the changes at all, while others thought things were not changing fast enough. Gorbachev was openly criticized and heckled when he spoke in public. The republics that made up the USSR demanded their independence.

On August 19, 1991, a group of hard-line communists tried to overthrow Gorbachev. At the time, Mikhail and Raisa Gorbachev were on vacation in the Crimea. Members of the **KGB** put them under house arrest. In Moscow, the **coup** leaders sent tanks onto the streets, but ordinary people confronted the soldiers and asked them to leave. Boris Yeltsin, the president of Russia, called for Gorbachev to be released. On August 21, the leaders of the coup gave themselves up and were imprisoned. Gorbachev returned to Moscow looking tired and anxious.

Yeltsin made it clear that he had been responsible for saving Gorbachev. Yeltsin wanted to see the end of communism, so he forced Gorbachev to ban the Communist Party. By December 1991, the USSR had broken up. All of its fifteen

People in Moscow plead with a tank driver not to support the coup against Gorbachev in August 1991.

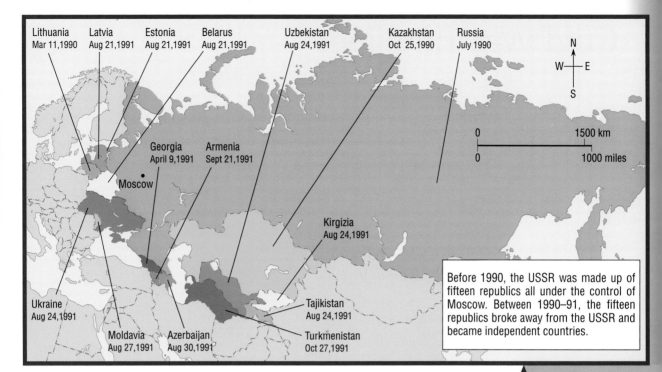

Kazakhstan Oct 25,1990 — Russia July 1990

N · W—E · S

0 — 1500 km
0 — 1000 miles

Georgia April 9,1991 — Armenia Sept 21,1991

Moscow

Kirgizia Aug 24,1991

Before 1990, the USSR was made up of fifteen republics all under the control of Moscow. Between 1990–91, the fifteen republics broke away from the USSR and became independent countries.

Ukraine Aug 24,1991

Tajikistan Aug 24,1991

Moldavia Aug 27,1991 — Azerbaijan Aug 30,1991 — Turkmenistan Oct 27,1991

member republics had declared themselves independent. On December 25, Gorbachev announced his resignation as Soviet president. As he spoke, the red flag with the hammer and sickle was lowered over the Kremlin. As Russia was the most powerful republic of the old USSR, its president, Yeltsin, was now in control of the nuclear weapons.

This map shows the rapid breakup of the USSR, 1990–91. The date of each republic's independence is shown after its name.

The world since the Cold War

Despite the ending of the Cold War, the world is not free of nuclear weapons. The United States, Russia, Britain, and France still possess long-range missiles. In 1998, both India and Pakistan carried out nuclear tests. So, though less likely than during the Cold War years, the possibility of a **nuclear war** is still with us.

After the Berlin Wall came down, West and East Germany became one country again, but problems remain. East Germans have their freedom and can vote in free elections, but people in the old West Germany are critical of how much taxpayers' money has been spent on the East; people in the East see themselves as poor relations. It has been harder to mold the two Germanys into one nation than people imagined.

In the old communist countries, **democracy** has not brought an end to poverty. The Czech Republic, Hungary, Poland, and Romania want to be full members of the **European Union (EU).** This will bring them into a family of **democratic** nations and enable them to build up trading links.

So the Cold War's demise has not brought a perfect world, but at least the cloud of extreme mistrust, suspicion, and paranoia between the East and West has been lifted. It remains to be seen what the future holds.

Cold War Timeline

	KEY EVENTS	ARMS RACE and SPACE RACE	U.S. PRESIDENTS	SOVIET LEADERS
1945	Yalta and Potsdam conferences, 1945 Churchill's "Iron Curtain" speech, 1946 Truman Doctrine and Marshall Plan, 1947 Berlin blockade and airlift, 1948–49 NATO formed, 1949	U.S. drops atomic bombs on Hiroshima and Nagasaki, Japan, 1945 USSR explodes an atomic bomb, 1949	Harry S. Truman (1945–53)	Josef Stalin [died 1953]
1950	Korean War, 1950–53	First hydrogen bomb (United States), 1952		
1955	Warsaw Pact formed, 1955 Revolt in Hungary against the USSR, 1956	*Sputnik 1*—first satellite (USSR), 1957	Dwight D. Eisenhower (1953–61)	Nikita Krushchev (1953–64)
1960	U-2 spy plane crisis, 1960 Berlin Wall goes up, 1961 Cuban Missile Crisis, 1962 Kennedy visits Berlin, 1963	Yuri Gagarin (USSR) orbits Earth, 1961 Test Ban Treaty, 1963	John F. Kennedy (1961–63)	
1965	Operation Rolling Thunder (Vietnam), 1965 Prague Spring; start of détente, 1968	Non-Proliferation Treaty, 1968 First men on the moon (United States), 1969	Lyndon B. Johnson (1963–69)	Leonid Brezhnev (1964–82)
1970	United States pulls troops out of Vietnam, 1973	SALT I, 1972	Richard M. Nixon (1969–74)	
1975	Helsinki agreement, 1975	Joint U.S./Soviet space mission, 1975	Gerald Ford (1974–77)	
1980	USSR invades Afghanistan; end of détente, 1979 United States boycotts Moscow Olympics, 1980	SALT II, 1979 (canceled 1980) SDI (Star Wars) announced by United States, 1983	Jimmy Carter (1977–81)	
1985	USSR boycotts Los Angeles Olympics, 1984 Reykjavik summit, 1986 Reagan visits Moscow, 1988		Ronald Reagan (1981–89)	Yuri Andropov (1982–84) Konstantin Chernenko (1984–85) Mikhail Gorbachev (1985–91)
1990	Berlin Wall comes down; end of Cold War, 1989 Breakup of the USSR, 1990		George H. W. Bush (1989–93)	

Map of the Cold War Hot Spots

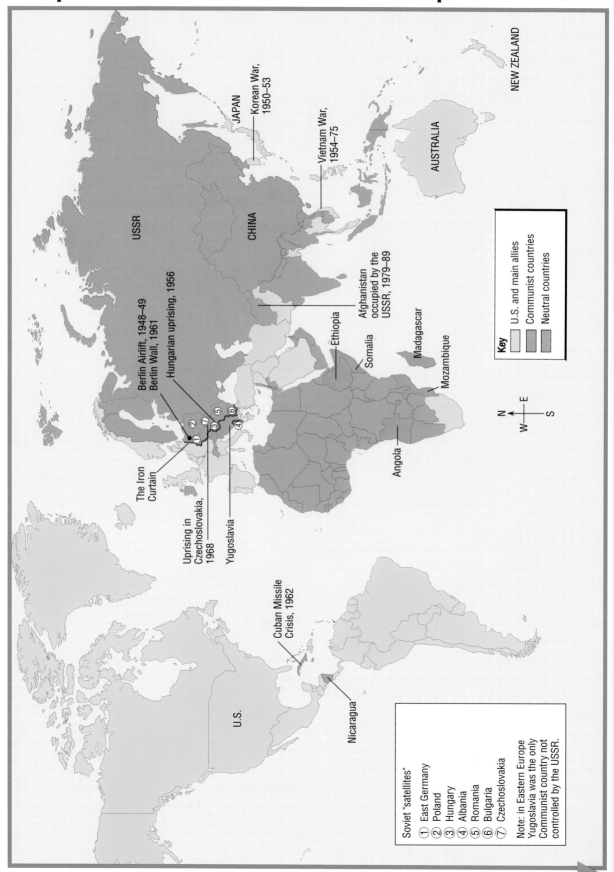

NEW ZEALAND

JAPAN

Korean War, 1950–53

Vietnam War, 1954–75

AUSTRALIA

USSR

CHINA

Afghanistan occupied by the USSR, 1979–89

Ethiopia

Somalia

Madagascar

Mozambique

Berlin Airlift, 1948–49
Berlin Wall, 1961

Hungarian uprising, 1956

Angola

The Iron Curtain

Uprising in Czechoslovakia, 1968

Yugoslavia

Cuban Missile Crisis, 1962

U.S.

Nicaragua

Key
- U.S. and main allies
- Communist countries
- Neutral countries

N E S W

Soviet "satellites"
1 East Germany
2 Poland
3 Hungary
4 Albania
5 Romania
6 Bulgaria
7 Czechoslovakia

Note: in Eastern Europe Yugoslavia was the only Communist country not controlled by the USSR.

More Books to Read

Nonfiction

Cheney, Glenn Alan. *Nuclear Proliferation: The Problems and Possibilities.* Danbury, Conn.: Franklin Watts, Inc., 1999.

Grant, R.G. *The Berlin Wall.* Austin, Tex.: Raintree Steck-Vaughn, 1998.

Kallen, Stuart A. *Gorbachev/Yeltsin: The Fall of Communism.* Edina, Minn.:ABDO, 1992.

Kelly, Nigel. *The Fall of the Berlin Wall.* Chicago: Heinemann Library, 2000.

Kelly, Nigel. *The Moon Landing.* Chicago: Heinemann Library, 2000.

Sherrow, Victoria. *Joseph McCarthy and the Cold War.* Woodbridge, Conn.: Blackbirch Press, 1998.

Shuter, Jane. *Russia and the USSR.* Chicago: Heinemann Library, 1996.

Stein, Conrad R. *The Great Red Scare.* Columbus, Ohio: Silver Burdett Press, 1997.

Warren, James A. *Cold War: The American Crusade Against the Soviet Union & World Communism.* Fairfield, N.J.: Lothrop, Lee & Shepard Books, 1996.

Fiction

Degens, T. *Freya on the Wall.* New York: Harcourt Trade Publishers, 1997.

Schneider, Peter. *The Wall Jumper: A Berlin Story.* Chicago: University of Chicago Press, 1998.

Glossary

allies countries who fight together for a common purpose

attorney general chief officer of the law in the United States who heads the Department of Justice

Bolshevik Party political party led by Vladimir Lenin that seized control of Russia in 1917

capitalism system which uses private wealth to produce goods

censoring when a government checks newspapers, television programs, and movies and removes material it does not want published

communism system in which the state owns all means of wealth production

Congress law-making body of the United States, made up of the House of Representatives and the Senate

conventional weapons non-nuclear weapons

coup takeover of a country by a small group, usually by violent means

cruise missiles long-range U.S. nuclear missiles

defectors people who desert a country

democracy government by elected representatives

Democratic Party one of the two main political parties in the United States; generally supports more government presence in people's lives

détente the relaxing of tension between the East and West

dissidents people who disagree strongly with the policies of a government

European Union (EU) group of European countries that trades freely with each other and shares a common defense policy

guerrillas small groups of soldiers who spring surprise attacks on the enemy

intelligence gathering of secret military information by spies

KGB Soviet secret police; its full name in Russian is the *Komitet Gosudarstvennoy Bezopasnosti*, which means "Committee for State Security"

Mujaheddin Muslim guerrilla fighters in Afghanistan who believe that the country should be ruled according to strict Muslim religious rules

Nazi led by Adolf Hitler, the Nazis (National Socialist Workers' Party) controlled Germany from 1933–45

nuclear warfare war using either atomic bombs or hydrogen bombs

pacifist person who does not believe in fighting wars

propaganda information to make people believe certain ideas or viewpoints

Quakers members of the Society of Friends, a religious group that believes in pacifism

radiation sickness illnesses caused by the fallout from a nuclear explosion

RAF British Royal Air Force

rationing when the supply of food is limited and controlled

Red Army army of the USSR

Republican Party one of the two main political parties in the United States, it favors big business and is against the government interfering in people's lives

Russian Civil War war fought between the Reds (communists) and Whites (supporters of Czar Nicholas II) from 1918 to 1921; it was won by the Reds

Russian Revolution communist seizure of power in Russia in 1917

satellite country that is dominated by a larger, more powerful country

secretary of state person in the U.S. government who is responsible for foreign affairs

second front opening of another fighting front in Western Europe during World War II when Britain and the United States invaded France on June 6, 1944. The first front was opened in 1941, when Nazi Germany invaded the USSR.

superpower name for the United States and the USSR, who emerged from World War II as the two most powerful countries in the world

totalitarian when one political party rules a country, banning other political parties and free speech

Union of Soviet Socialist Republics (USSR) first created in 1923 by the union of four republics: Russia, the Ukraine, Belarus, and the Caucasus. It grew to include fifteen communist republics. It broke up in 1991.

United Nations (UN) association of countries formed after World War II to work for world peace

USAF United States Air Force

Vietcong communist guerrilla who fought the Americans in South Vietnam

Vietminh shortened name for the League for the Independence of Vietnam, formed in 1941 by Ho Chi Minh

Watergate biggest political scandal in U.S. history, brought about when five men hired by the Republican Party broke into the Watergate complex in Washington D.C., in 1972, the headquarters of the Democratic Party. The scandal led to the resignation of President Richard Nixon in 1974.

Index